The World of AMPHIBIANS and REPTILES

BY MILLI UBERTAZZI TANARA

TRANSLATED FROM THE ITALIAN BY Simon Pleasance

GALLERY BOOKS
An Imprint of W. H. Smith Publishers Inc.
112 Madison Avenue
New York City 10016

Designers/Artists
Illustrations drawn by Remo Squillantini together with the following:
Piero Cozzaglio, Brescia: 11, 24, 88, 89, 107, 126b, 138a, 139, 227. Raffaele
Curiel, Verona: 38. Raffaello Segattini, Verona: 27ad, 31, 32d, 33, 37s, 39,
41, 45s, 46a, 47, 48, 52a, 53, 63ad/bs, 79, 85, 86–87, 90, 92, 104–105, 107a,
109a, 111, 113b, 115, 118, 120, 121a, 123, 124a, 125, 136a, 137, 140–141b,
142, 145a, 148, 150, 156a, 157, 160d, 162, 171cs/cd, 180, 183, 194, 195, 197,
208, 220d, 222, 225a, 226, 227ad, 238, 244, 245.

Photographs
Archivio Mondadori, Milan: 185, Ardea Photographics, London: Su Good-
ers: 169. G. Carles/G. Lolivier, Paris: 99, 144, 219. Jacana, Paris: Bailleau:
204; Brosset: 192; Chaumeton 20b, 22, 173s; Chevreuil: 46b; Devez: 61,
91a; Dubois: 100b; Hladik: 207; Lanceau: 167, 217; Lelo: 240–241; Nardin:
160b, 212; Renaud: 64–65; Stiegler: 115b; Summ: 143; Tercais: 32s; Thib-
out: 218, 236; Vasserot: 108, 133, 145b, 178, 186; Vial: 173d; Visage: 113,
135. Aldo Margiocco, Genova: 144, 155bs, 184, 201, 237. Marka Graphic,
Milan: Schulz-Guidon: 6–7. Guiseppe Mazza, Milan: 19b, 36, 42, 43a, 57,
172d. Pieter, Milan: 74a, 80, 81, 110b. Mauro Pucciarelli, Rome: 199. Folco
Quilici, Rome: 193. Luisa Ricciarini, Milan: B. Lanza: 23b, 52b, 63bd, 86; G.
Leonardi: 91b; Sandro Prato: 179; Enrico Febba: 187; Gustavo Tomsich:
37d, 43b. Prof. H. Saint Girons, Paris: 151, 153a, 190, 206, 211. Union Press,
Milan: 165. U.S. National Museum, Washington: 121b. Prof. R. G. Zweifeld,
New York: 200.

Library of Congress Cataloging in Publication Data

Ubertazzi Tanara, Milly.
THE WORLD OF AMPHIBIANS AND REPTILES.

Translation of Il mondo degli anfibi e dei rettili.
Bibliography: p. 252–3
1. Amphibians. 2. Reptiles. I. Title.
OL644.T3613   598.1   79-1441

ISBN: 0-8317-9551–4

Printed and bound in Italy by Officine Grafiche of Arnoldo
Mondadori Editore, Verona.

This edition published by Gallery Books, a division of W.H. Smith Inc.,
112 Madison Avenue, New York, New York 10016.
Originally published by Abbeville Press, Inc.

Contents

Amphibians

Introduction

Take any remote day, 350,000,000 years ago: life on our planet seemed to have reached a state of relative peace and quiet. The oceans seethed with extremely varied forms of animal and plant life, the land above sea-level was being colonized by increasingly lush vegetation, and the ponds, marshes and lagoons housed an ever-growing number of invertebrate inhabitants. It was in these latter aquatic environments that a very interesting series of phenomena started to appear. Every time a pond or lagoon dried up during a period of drought, its inhabitants were faced with three options: they could adapt themselves for a return to the sea, or bury themselves in the residual mud and wait for the water to return, or somehow make their way to *terra firma* and try to reach another pond. The first creatures to opt for the last solution were certain members of the order Rhipidistia, a group of lobe-finned bony fish not unlike lung-fish. The terrestrial migration by these fish to new and perhaps less densely populated waters led to increased terrestrial adaptations, like internal nostrils.

The first problem encountered by these fish was to find

enough food, despite the dry conditions, and to do this it was vital to be able to move about on dry land as well. Among Vertebrates, fish were unable to perfect that whole series of adaptations necessary for life on dry land. The animals which achieved a certain independence from the aquatic habitat in this same period (known as the Middle Palaeozoic period) were more 'recent' forms, whose body-structure bore certain resemblances to their forebears, the Rhipidistia. These were the so-called Ichthyostegalia. Fossil remains tell us that it had a short trunk about one metre in length, with a tough tail fin supported by bony rays; the vertebrae were simple and the skull was formed by numerous bones, similar to the skull of Rhipidistians.

However, unlike the Rhipidistians, the *Ichthyostega* had already developed limbs capable of raising the body above the ground. For this salamander-like creature, walking on all fours was the first step towards a permanent adaptation to dry land. It was also the founder of the large family of toads, frogs, newts, salamanders and a few other animals classed together as

Amphibia. Even today, these creatures seem to repeat the various stages of that distant conquest of the land. The actual name given to this class indicates as much. The word 'amphibian' in Greek means 'double life' (from *amphi* – αμφι – double, and *bios* – βios – life) referring to the fact that for almost all these animals, life can be clearly divided into two phases. First, an aquatic, larval phase, which starts as soon as the egg opens, and then a terrestrial, adult phase, lived for the most part on dry land. The progression from one form of life to the next is accompanied by a series of transformations which affect both the structure and the functioning of the organs of these animals.

Returning to the ancestors of present-day amphibians, it can be maintained that in the latter stages of the Palaeozoic Era these were the animals best suited to life on Earth, and also the best represented in a numerical sense. This was because in those remote days the amphibians had no rivals vying for space, food and shelter. The evolutionary process which led from those primitive Ichthyostegalia to the present-day amphibians was neither immediate nor direct and many forms appeared and then died out, leaving just a few fossils to testify to their existence. This happened in the case of the long-tailed Embolomeri (their tails grew up to 4 metres in length!) which were flattened laterally and also in the case of the monstrous Rhachitomi, which had armour-plated skeletons, and the gigantic Stereospondylii, which were very widespread in inland waters and grew to a truly colossal size for creatures in this class. The Mastodonsaurus, which existed in Europe during the Triassic Era (some 220,000,000 years ago), had a skull which measured 1.25 metres in height. It has been suggested that *Triadobatrachus*, which appeared in the Triassic Era, may have been an ancestral form of the Anura. Fossils have been discovered in Madagascar showing that the skull had a small number of bones, the tail was long and the hindlegs were fairly well developed, although apparently not capable of jumping. The Caudata (amphibians with tails such as newts, salamanders and the like) probably had the same ancestors as the Anura. The apodous, or legless, amphibians (Gymnophiona) with their typically worm-shaped bodies, may not be as closely related to the other amphibians as was once believed and may have quite separate ancestry.

Mention should be made of the famous cretaceous fossil *Andrias* found in Germany in 1726, because of the misunderstanding caused by its discovery. At the time it was mistaken for the skeleton of a child who was thought to have died at the time of the Flood, and was taken to be irrefutable proof of the truth of the biblical tale. It was not until much later, however, that scholars were able to confirm that it was the skeleton of an animal, and classify it as belonging to a species of huge salamander. It was the discovery by the naturalist Schlegel of the giant Japanese salamander

Skeleton of
Miobatrachus ▶

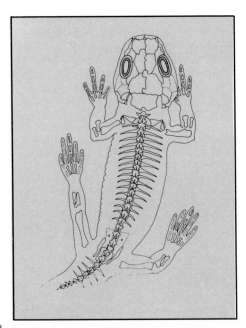

▼ Skeleton of *Ichthyostega*

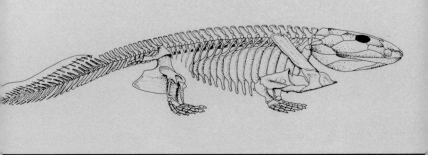

(*Negalobatrachus japonicus*) that confirmed the existence of this enormous amphibian many millions of years ago.

There are about 2400 species of amphibians currently living on the Earth, divided into three orders which all have distinctive specific features: the order Gymnophiona (legless amphibians) found in tropical regions, with a cylindrical and often very elongated body, no legs, and adapted to a terrestrial if not subterranean existence, and in a few cases aquatic life; the Caudata, with a well-developed tail both in the larval and adult phases; and the Anura, which are short-bodied, tail-less as adults, with fairly strong hind legs suited to jumping.

Taken as a whole, this class of Vertebrates offers a feature of interest and importance. Despite the numerous geological and climatic changes undergone by the Earth between the Palaeozoic Era and today, the small present-day members of the group are very similar in the structure and organization of their bodies to their distant forebears. Throughout their evolution they have evidently equipped themselves in the most appropriate way to deal with life in environments subject to periodic climatic variations.

Amphibians have always disliked saltwater and either consistently cold or dry climates. However, they will live quite happily at high altitudes (some species of frogs live at altitudes of 4500 metres in the Andes and Himalayas, where it is almost continually under snow) and in the darkness of underground burrows or caves. Should there be sudden climatic changes such as an unexpected bout of dry weather, some of these creatures have developed specialised techniques which enable them to survive. For instance, some will adopt a huddled position which minimizes the surface exposed to the air and thus reduces the danger of losing excessive amounts of water. Some will emit from their skin a secretion which ensures that the creature will remain constantly moist, and some will try to conserve this precious fluid by preferably leading a nocturnal existence.

A final unusual aspect of the members of this class is the fact that their history is often associated with that of witches, sorcerers and magicians. Their blood and the poisons produced by them were vital ingredients of potions alleged to have miraculous powers.

Salamanders, more than other amphibians, have always been associated with legendary tales. The Greeks, for instance, believed that these creatures could live in fire. This mistaken idea which commonly held for so long still lingers on in some quarters, where people are naive enough to think that these small creatures are fire resistant. People have even believed that a fire could be put out by throwing a salamander into it. In Ancient Rome, and in the Middle Ages, these 'living extinguishers' were often sold as precautions against fire.

Similarly the ability to re-grow a partly or completely snapped-off leg or tail, and the ability to produce excess digits or limbs has greatly contributed to the reputation enjoyed by amphibians as extraordinary creatures.

Despite all such beliefs and superstitions, the Amphibians undoubtedly occupy an important position on the Vertebrates' evolutionary ladder. In fact they are the concrete evidence of the progression from a fairly simple type of life (the life of fish) to the evolution of reptiles, birds and mammals.

▼ Marsh frog *Rana ridibunda*

Structure

Shapes and sizes

Although the amphibians fall into three clearly defined morphological groups – the Gymnophiona, Caudata or Anura – they also come in a fairly vast range of shapes and sizes which are for the most part related to their environment or habitat. This habitat is more accurately described as the micro-habitat, because the areas involved are generally limited in size.

The Gymnophiona (sometimes but incorrectly referred to as Apoda) have a distinctive body which is almost cylindrical in shape, worm-like, and legless, because these creatures mostly live underground. It also has a soft glandular skin which is furrowed by a series of very close ring-like grooves. In fact the untrained eye might easily mistake these amphibians for common earth-worms. The Caudata include all the amphibians that have tails both in the larval stage and as adults. They have flattened heads, long bodies, and legs which are sometimes so weak that they have difficulty in supporting the body which is usually dragged clumsily along the ground.

Within this Order, however, there are certain species whose

outward morphology sets them apart from the typical member of the Caudata. These are the siren, the lesser siren and the pseudobranchus, all belonging to the family Sirenidae; the congo eel (*Amphiuma means*) and the three-toed amphiuma (*A. tridactylum*) belonging to the family Amphiumidae; and the Californian slender salamander belonging to the huge family Plethodontidae. All these animals have long, snake-like bodies (the siren measures up to 90 cm) or short snake-like bodies (the worm salamander varies between 90–130 mm) with a small diameter, and poorly developed, or in some cases non-existent, limbs. In the case of the Sirenidae, for example, there are a reduced number of toes.

Finally there are the Anura, the so-called jumping amphibians. As adults these have squat, tail-less bodies, with the exception of the *Ascaphus truei*, which is commonly known as the tailed frog. Here the adult male has an odd, small stump at the end of its trunk which it uses to transfer sperm to the female. The head is large; the legs, and the hind legs in particular, are well developed for swimming and jumping, which are the two types of movement that enable the tailed frog to move in water and on dry land.

Similarly among the Anura there are forms that differ from the typical appearance of the Order. For example the African clawed toad belonging to the family Pipidae has a very flattened, hydrodynamic body and eyes set on top of the head in an almost horizontal position; the Malayan or Asian horned toad (Pelobatidae) has a face which appears to be 'deformed' by the presence of long skin flaps on both the eyelids and the tip of the nose; the South African rain frog (Brericeps gibbasus), belonging to the Microhylidae has, as its common name suggests, a spherical body like a swollen bladder, a small, pointed face, and stumpy legs which are useless for swimming.

One of the most interesting aspects of almost all amphibians is, of course, the series of radical changes undergone by most of them when they pass from the larval to the adult stage. The larval forms are in fact usually aquatic, so the form of their bodies must be such as to make their existence in this type of habitat as simple as possible. For this reason the larva of the Caudata and the tadpoles of the Anura have fish-shaped bodies with fairly pronounced tails, round heads generally with gills at the sides for breathing, and no legs, at least in the early stages of growth. Metamorphosis (which is the series of changes undergone by the various organs which marks the transition from the aquatic life of the larva, to the life on dry land of the adult) radically alters the outward appearance of both these types of larvae, although in several species of Caudata the appearance of the animal remains larval. In other words the animal reaches adult size and full sexual development, but still breathes by means of external gills and leads a totally aquatic life. The olm (*Proteus anguineus*) which lives in caves and in the water-bearing strata of the Adriatic coast is the best known example of this phenomenon. Its slender white body, between 23–25 cm in length, is tapered and ends in a flattened tail; its limbs are extremely short and fingers and toes are reduced in number; the gills are external and red in colour, and thus easy to see because they stand out sharply from the total absence of colour in the rest of the body.

The Mexican salamander (*Ambystoma mexicanum*) also has a 'neotenic' shape (this is the term given to animals which, though sexually mature, keep their gills and their larval appearance) which is very distinctive. In about the mid-19th century a strange thing happened to this creature. Up until that time it had been considered, as a larva, as a clearly defined species, and classified as such. In reality the axolotl in the

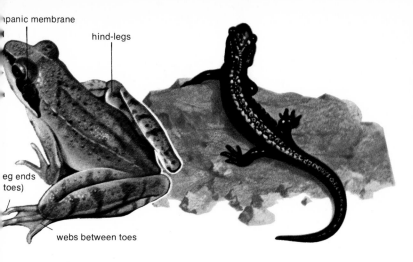

panic membrane

hind-legs

eg ends
toes)

webs between toes

▲ Outward appearance of an anuran (frog) and a caudata (salamander)

aquarium in the Jardin des Plantes in Paris was just the neotenic form of the ordinary salamander called *Ambystoma mexicanum*. Zoologists were able to confirm this during one fine day when their axolotl started its metamorphosis: the brightly coloured gills were absorbed, the colour of the body turned from grey to speckled yellow; its aquatic habits were forgotten, and it did not return to the water until the following spring, for the mating season. One of the features common to almost all the lower vertebrates (in other words to fishes, amphibians and reptiles) is the fact that they continue to grow throughout their life. Thus the largest specimens are also the oldest. Of course until sexual maturity is reached growth in young specimens is quick, and becomes slower and slower in adults, although it never stops altogether.

The largest of all present-day amphibians belong to the family Cryptobranchidae in the Order Caudata. The animals concerned are four species of aquatic salamanders found in the Far East (the Japanese giant salamander and the Chinese giant salamander) and on the North American continent (the hellbender and the *Cryptobranchus bishopi*). The largest of these is the Japanese species which can reach a length of 1.6 m, followed by the Chinese species and then the North American species. Another member of the Caudata, which lives on dry land and has a somewhat flattened body, is found in Spain, Portugal and Morocco. This is the *Pleurodeles* which can reach a length of 30 and even 40 cm. Apart from these few exceptions the average dimensions of the adult Caudata vary

17

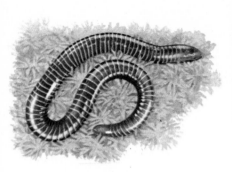

▲ Mikan's Caecilian
Siphonops annulatus

▲ The olm *Proteus anguinus*

between 5 and 20 cm, and in the terrestrial forms the body and the tail in particular tend to be elongated.

As far as the Anura are concerned, tadpoles are almost always smaller than their respective adult forms, but members of the family Pseudidae have larvae which grow almost out of all proportion and far exceed the size of the adults. As a result their metamorphosis involves a reduction in the size of the organs rather than their continued development. The Paradoxical frog (*Pseudis paradoxa*), which is found on the island of Trinidad and in the Amazon basin, has tadpoles which can reach a length of 25 cm, whereas the adults rarely measure more than 75 mm.

Other tiny Anura include the African sedge frogs, and the *Hyperolius horstock*. The latter, for example, measures just 25 mm, and can easily hide itself inside the spathe of a water lily, but most of the 'micro-amphibians' belong to the family Leptodactylidae. Good examples are the tiny swamp-dwelling species in the genus *Pseudopaludicola*, which are about 18 mm long and can make very nimble hops sideways; Girard's frog (*Zachaenus parvulus*), which is also about 18 mm long and fairly aggressive; the notorious *vaquero* which lives in the forests of Chile and has the strange habit of hatching its larvae in its mouth, and is just 25 mm long. The smallest of all is the Cuban *Sminthillus limbatus* belonging to the family Dendrobatidae, which in the adult stage measures just slightly more than 12 mm.

18

Marine toad *Bufo marinus*

The Japanese giant salamander *Andrias japonicus* can grow to 1.60 m

East African tree frog
Hylambates maculatus ▶

▲ The skin of an amphibian at the moment of shedding

The skin and its features

The skin of any amphibian, be it a member of the Gymnophiona, Caudata or Anura, looks bare, sometimes smooth, perhaps covered with warts, usually slimy to the touch. It may change colour depending on the surroundings, the time of day, the time of life or sexual development; most of these features are acquired by all the various members of the class. In fact many of the ancient Ichthyostegalia had a bony dermoskeleton covered with scales and plates, probably to protect the skeleton and the internal organs from the various dangers in the habitat, and from a climate with which they were still not very familiar. It is known that some of the members of the order Gymnophiona – perhaps the oldest of all the amphibians – still retain this primitive feature. While the skin of some of the primitive caecilians looks smooth and slimy, it has various cycloid scales embedded in the skin.

Because the skin is involved in the breathing of these creatures, it is always thin, permeable and moist. The moisture is produced by mucus which in turn is produced by a large number of glands. These mucous glands, together with other larger and more numerous glands, are situated beneath the skin and scattered more or less all over the body.

The mucous glands work continuously, and more actively when exposed to hot, dry air. They emit a clear fluid which covers the body with a layer of mucus. The other glands, on the other hand, work more intermittently. If there should be a period of prolonged drought, they produce a thick fluid which is whitish in colour and contains a high proportion of poisonous substances. These glands are usually concentrated in strands, warts and various other forms of conglomeration. The males of certain species of Anura have a third type of gland situated on the inside of the first finger and sometimes on the second finger too which has a sexual function: the fluid emitted by these glands enables them to hold the female more tightly during mating, and the gland is often cornified or spiny to increase the grip.

In many cases the skin emits distinctive smells. In certain cases, as in the case of the Plethodontidae among the Caudata, it acts as a sexual lure, and is found specifically in males. In other cases this phenomenon is a symptom of fear. If pursued, the common spadefoot toad covers itself with a secretion which smells of garlic. Many North American toads produce an exudate which smells of pepper and mould at one and the same time. Toads and salamanders may smell slightly of vanilla and if they are annoyed this smell becomes much more pungent.

21

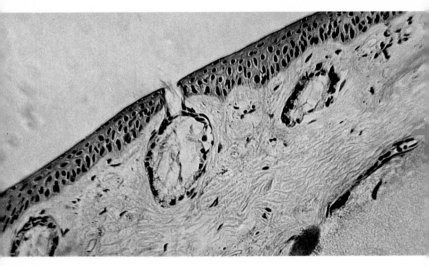

▲ Cross section of skin of an amphibian showing mucous glands

The skin of amphibians comes in a very wide variety of colours. As well as shades of green and brown, which reflect the main hues of the surrounding vegetation, there are shades of red, blue, yellow, violet and black.

These colours are the work of special skin cells known as chromatophores which contain dark or light pigments. The chromatophores are star-shaped and with variations in temperature, light and ambient humidity can contract or expand and thus produce temporary variations in the colour of the skin.

Amphibians are periodically subject to the phenomenon of shedding their skin. It is discarded like a piece of clothing that has become too tight. Beneath it a new skin is formed which is better suited to the increased size of the creature. The 'techniques' used by the various species also differ: newts peel off their old skin from front to back, using their legs; other species rub their bodies against rocks or plants to help the exuviae become detached (this is the scientific term for the old skin), and the old skin then breaks up into small bits on its own; and yet others make the old skin tear apart by making a series of movements like swallowing. The shed skin is then almost invariably eaten because it contains nutritious substances which it would be wasteful to reject.

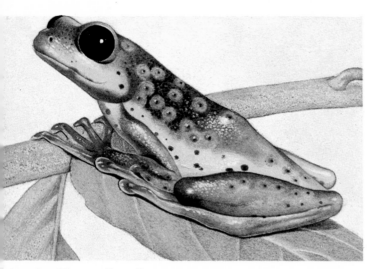

A species of the genus *Hyperolius*

Variation in the dorsal colouration of salamanders

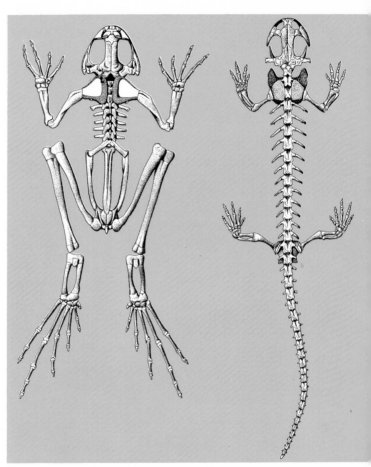

▲ The skeleton of a frog (Anura)   ▲ The skeleton of a salamander (Caudata

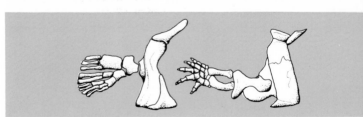

The scapular girdle and fin or flipper ▲
of a member of the Crossopterygii

▲ The scapular girdle and fro[n]
leg of a primitive amphibian

The skeleton and musculature

As in all vertebrates, the axis of the body in this class is represented by the spinal column which is formed by vertebrae. The number of vertebrae varies from Order to Order. In the Anura there are never more than nine, in the Caudata it may be as many as 100, and in the Gymnophiona it can be as high as 250. On the basis of their shape the vertebrae are classified as procoelous (if they are concave on the front face), opisthocoelous (if they are concave behind) and amphicoelous (if they are biconcave). There is no rib-cage, but if, as in primitive frogs, the adult animal has ribs they are short and generally fused to spinal processes and never reach the sternum. The cranium is joined to the spinal column by means of two condyles and is generally broad and flat. Here the ear aperture appears for the first time. This is closed off by the membrane of the eardrum which is derived from the spiracle in fish. There are usually four limbs which are derived from the transformation of the paired lobed fins of the Crossopterygii. They consist of a tough, short humerus, and femur (arm and thigh-bone) which are positioned horizontally, while the radius and ulna (for the front legs) and the tibia and fibula (for the hind legs), which are also short and tough, are on a vertical plane, in order to keep the body raised above the ground. The pectoral and pelvic girdles attach the limbs to the spinal column.

The Gymnophiona in particular have a skeleton formed by amphicoelous vertebrae, short ribs, though better developed than in the other members of the class; a fairly elongated compact cranium which is made up of very toughened bones to enable the animal to burrow in the ground, but no legs.

The Caudata, on the other hand, have a spinal column formed by amphicoelous and opisthocoelous vertebrae, short ribs, and strong girdles capable of supporting the limbs. But the legs are not very strong, and generally end in four toes in the front limbs and five in the hind legs. There are exceptions to this rule: the Sirenidae and the Amphiumidae with their two- or three-toed legs; the *Manculus* and slimy salamander with four-toed feet all round; and the olm which has three fingers on the front legs and two on the hind legs.

The Anura have a short skeleton, and apart from primitive forms the adults are ribless. They also have strong girdles to support the four legs. The front legs have four toes and the hind legs five. The hind legs are better developed than the front limbs. Because the cranium is attached to the spinal column by two condyles the head has very limited movement.

The anatomy of the edible frog *Rana esculenta*

▲ The European frog *Rana temporaria*

The internal organs

These organs complete the body structure. They are covered by the thin epidermis and the layer of muscles, and supported by or contained within the skeletal framework. Their functions are feeding and breathing, reproduction and coordination, and the conveyance of substances vital for the survival of the body cells and the elimination of waste. The fact that amphibians are Vertebrates, or Chordates (*Chordata*) – animals which in the earliest stages of development have a notochord which is later replaced by the spinal column – in some sense determines the internal organization of the bodies of the amphibians.

Because amphibians are subject to metamorphosis (or at least, in the case of the neotenic forms, to considerable structural modifications), account must be taken of the various habitats occurring in the various phases for each organ and system, as well as the functions carried out by them. Thus for breathing, the gills of aquatic larvae are invariably replaced by lungs in the adults forms. Similarly, the blood, which in larvae and tadpoles is conveyed by a rudimentary circulatory system, runs in proper blood-vessels in adults, and is pumped round by a proper heart. The adults' diet is no longer vegetarian but becomes carnivorous, and thus the organs for feeding become more complex.

26

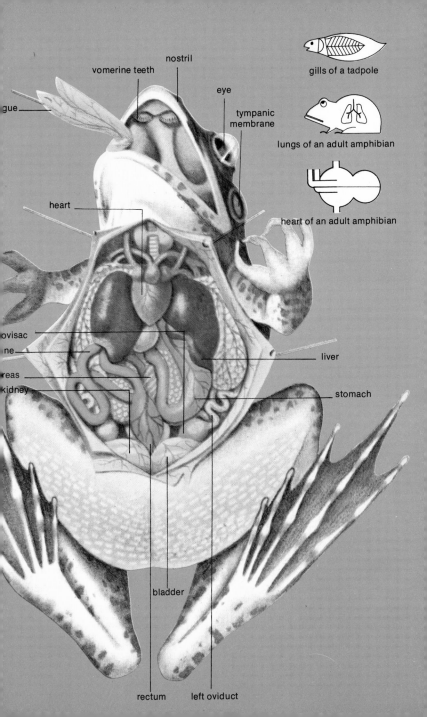

nostril

vomerine teeth

eye

tympanic membrane

gue

heart

ovisac

ne

reas

kidney

liver

stomach

bladder

rectum

left oviduct

gills of a tadpole

lungs of an adult amphibian

heart of an adult amphibian

How Amphibians Live

Life in the water

For the most part amphibians are generally aquatic animals at birth, and as such spend their early days in the water. However, there comes a time when amphibians are forced to abandon their watery surroundings and confront life in a new environment where the principal feature is the fact that it is dry. From this day onward water will only play an occasional rôle, and in some cases it will actually have to be reconquered, often at considerable expense. Like the fishes which had preceded them on the evolutionary ladder and the reptiles which come after them, the amphibians are first and foremost poikilothermic (or cold-blooded) animals in which the body temperature varies with the temperature of the environment outside. When it is cold all activity slows down until a state of torpor is reached. When it is warm activity is increased. Unlike reptiles, for whom low temperatures cause periods of deep, lethargic sleep, amphibians can tolerate the cold better, especially in regions where the climate is very dry. In fact in low temperatures the relative humidity of the environment (that is the percentage of water

present in a cubic metre of air in the form of vapour) is enough to prevent their skin from drying up. Amphibians are thus quite capable of living both in very humid environments, such as swamps or equatorial forests, and in cool environments. Among the Caudata, many Hynobiidae are to be found in the cold but muddy tundra regions, on the Siberian border. High temperatures, on the other hand, often give rise to opportune periods of torpor. These periods of inactivity save the animal from the excessive heat and thus from the danger of serious dehydration. Water is therefore the limiting factor in the life of amphibians.

Feeding
Once the egg has opened, the very young larvae soon have to procure food on their own. This food is no longer at hand, but scattered in the water around them. To manage this, nature has equipped them with a fairly wide and appropriately designed mouth. The larvae of many Caudata prefer a carnivorous diet. These creatures usually prey on tiny invertebrates, the larvae of insects and crustaceans, and soft-shelled molluscs.

Their mouth does not generally have the small horny teeth of tadpoles, but jaws fitted with actual teeth which are thin and needle-sharp. The main task of these teeth is to hold on to the prey which is sucked into the mouth together with water. Obviously there are certain forms of larvae which have jaws with horny plates which are replaced after metamorphosis.

The Anura, on the other hand, at least as tadpoles, have a herbivorous diet. To this end their mouths are designed for rasping. In the middle of the mouth there is a microscopic horny 'beak' which is slightly hooked (like a miniature parrot's beak). All around the large lips many species have rows of small horny teeth shaped like rasps and arranged differently from one family or species to the next. After metamorphosis all these structures are gradually replaced by proper bony structures. Here too there are many variations on the basic theme. Among the Pelobatidae, certain species of *Megophrys* have tadpoles with 'umbrella'-like mouths, where the funnel-shaped lips have many small, rasping, horny teeth arranged around them like so many spokes. The tadpoles of this species swim upright, as if 'suspended' from their large mouths, which act as buoys. In certain aquatic frogs found in ponds and pools in southern Asia the mouth is by contrast small and surrounded by a horseshoe-shaped, toothless lip with a sort of rasping, horny rostrum or beak at the centre. A particularly interesting feature in the tadpoles of the genus *Xenopus* is the filtering mechanism, which is designed to retain small particles of food. At the sides of the pharynx, situated on the inner surface of the branchial arches, there is an actual filter through which the water sucked in by the mouth is expelled, while the food particles caught in it are conveyed to the intestinal canal. It should be mentioned that the structure, and above all the length of the intestine, are always in relation to the type of diet of the larvae. Thus the intestine of the Caudata, which are typically carnivorous animals, is not particularly long, whereas the intestines of the Anura, which are vegetarian, form an extremely long digestive system, which is wrapped over and over on itself in the shape of a spiral. The process of metamorphosis is invariably accompanied by an unravelling and shortening of the digestive system.

These are not the only changes required by life on dry land. The absorption of the gills, the closing of the branchial apertures, the cessation of the mechanisms of sucking in water and then filtering it which function at the first stage of the pharynx, are all determining factors as regards the structural characteristics which are essential for an adequate supply of

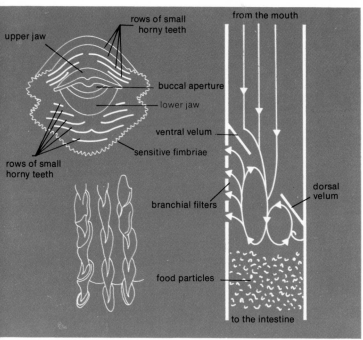

▲ Mouth and teeth of a tadpole

▲ Centrifugal flow and filters in the pharynx of a tadpole

food in adult animals within this class.

The mouth aperture of adult amphibians, and of the Anura in particular, is fairly large, so as to be able to hold other animals, intact and still alive, as prey.

In this second phase of their existence, the amphibians are all carnivorous, with certain preferences for particular 'specialities': not only insects, spiders and worms, but fishes, other amphibians, small reptiles, small mice and other small mammals all make up their daily diet. The Cryptobranchidae are the only amphibians that also feed on animal excrement. Certain Caudata of the genus *Aneides* have the strange habit of supplementing their carnivorous diet with fungi growing on the trunks of the trees in which they live. They manage to nibble the fungi by means of their strong teeth which are very sharp.

All amphibians catch their victims with lightning speed. Guided by their sense of smell they are able to single out the right prey for their palate, both in the water and on dry land. Depending on whether they have a tongue or not, the techniques used to do this are varied. For instance, the Gymnophiona (legless amphibians), many Caudata and certain Anura that do not have a tongue grab their victims directly with their powerful jaws. In animals that have tongues, this is the main instrument used for hunting. Certain Caudata have mushroom-shaped tongues. These are supported by a kind of mobile peduncle or stem, are sticky due to the plentiful mucus covering them, and can be thrust outwards, either partly or completely, depending how far away the prey is. In many Anura, and in frogs for example, the tongue is fixed to the bottom of the mouth in the foremost part, while the back margin is free and can be flipped over with a swift, sudden movement. The Mexican burrowing toad has a tongue rather like a mammal's; it is unattached at the front and only fixed at the back. The so-called 'narrow-mouthed toads' (Microhylidae) on the other hand have a slender tongue which

▼ Alpine newt
Triturus alpestris

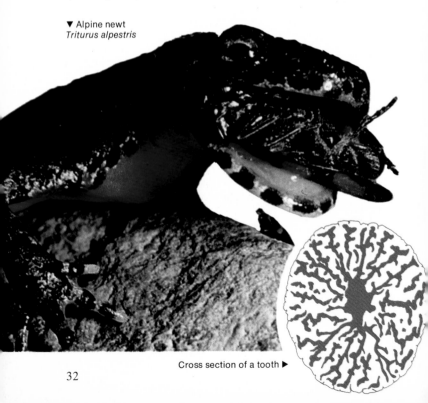

Cross section of a tooth ▶

is circular in section and fixed at its middle point so that it can be thrust towards the prey which is seized in this way. These Microhylidae feed mainly on ants and termites. The members of the family Pipidae were at one time defined as Aglossa (or Aglossinae) – tongue-less Anura; they are voracious to the point of cannibalism, in many cases devouring their own offspring, and eat almost any type of animal matter, alive or dead. One of them, the African clawed toad (*Xenopus*) has a rather comical way of pushing its food into its mouth: once the prey has been seized, it chews it quickly so as to kill it, and to do this it uses its two front legs which it brings alternately and very swiftly towards its mouth.

In the Caudata the small teeth are set in both the lower and upper jaws. One can identify a peduncle set in the bone and a crown with two cusps; between the peduncle and the crown these teeth have a fibrous type of horizontal ring, which is absent in the Sirenidae. A characteristic confined to the Caudata is that in the Sirenidae both jaws are tooth-less. In

▼ Projection of the mushroom-shaped tongue of genus *Hydromantes*

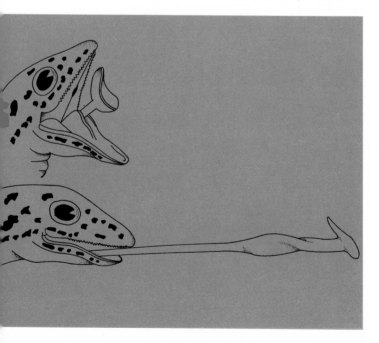

place of teeth they have nothing more than a horny layer which is similarly seen in certain larvae of Hynobiidae and Ambystomidae. In the Anura teeth are not always a constant feature. In many species, such as those belonging to the genera *Bufo* (the true toads), *Dendrobates* and *Phyllobates*, there are no teeth at all. Although most members of the order have teeth on both upper and lower jaws, plus two short rows in a palatal position, some species, for example the Neotropical marsupial frogs, lack teeth on the lower jaws and palate. However, when teeth are present they have a structure comparable to that of the Caudata and the Gymnophiona: a peduncle at the base, a crown on top and between the two a zone of weakness that allows the crown to be lost but prevents the entire tooth being shed. In some cases the absence of teeth is made up for by the appearance of certain 'odontoid' formations, which are bony in origin.

Still in connection with the mouth, mention should be made of the numerous glands which are hidden in the buccal epithelium all round the buccal aperture. These glands secrete a mucus to make the process of swallowing easier. It is also probable that they process digestive enzymes which, as in mammals, initiate the digestive process. Turning now to live prey, here too the operation of swallowing the prey is never a particularly simple one. Suffice it to say that in order to swallow an insect toads will even use the pressure which can be brought to bear on the mouthful by the eye-balls. Toads in fact swallow their prey with their eyes closed so that their eye-balls can be dropped on to the palate to push the food into the oesophagus or gullet.

As far as the Caudata are concerned it is the Plethodontidae that have a special system for swallowing. These animals have a fixed mandible and in order to chew and swallow they have to move their jaws, and with them their entire cranium.

After passing the oesophagus, the food travels along the alimentary canal, through the stomach, which can dilate to a remarkable extent, and then the intestine. The final outlet of the intestine is the cloaca, a cavity which also receives the ends of the excretory and genital organs.

Methods of breathing

Of all the modifications undergone by the amphibians during their life, the most important concerns the organs for breathing. However, the behaviour of the various members of the three orders in the class differs somewhat.

As larvae, the Gymnophiona may have thin branchial clefts

on the sides of their neck, or even lungs, depending on the species involved. In the case of the Caudata, the larvae breathe by means of external and ramified gills which are later re-absorbed in individuals that have undergone complete metamorphosis and which will remain for the entire life span in the neotenic forms. Lastly, the tadpoles of the Anura initially breathe through their skin. External gills appear in the second phase of development, and these in turn vanish as soon as the internal gills are formed. These latter are hidden by a cutaneous operculum and open outwards by means of the so-called spiracle (or kind of gill-slit), which consists of a siphon-like aperture through which the water which runs into the gills through the mouth is expelled. At the end of the process of metamorphosis the internal gills are in turn absorbed and the task of breathing then falls to the lungs (in addition to the skin, which is described later).

In the adult stage there are three different situations as follows: the Gymnophiona which are usually equipped with lungs; the Caudata which have long, narrow lungs typical of animals with elongated bodies, or external gills in the neotenic forms (the most glaring exception is represented by the Plethodontidae, which have no lungs at all and as a result breathe solely through their skin); the Anura almost all of which have sac-like lungs with thin walls, originating from two bronchial tubes.

Among the Leptodactylidae, the members of the genus *Telmatobius*, which live in icy lakes and rivers in the Andes, have no lungs whatsoever. In fact because some live on the oozy bottom of deep lakes, they have developed a baggy skin that acts as their respiratory organ. For these creatures lungs would be a hindrance because the air contained in them would cause them to float. Among the Ranidae the male hairy frog (*Trichobatracbus robustus*) of the Cameroons makes up for the mediocre efficiency of its lungs by having, during the breeding season, a series of thin, vascularized filaments on the sides of its trunk and thighs. These apparently act as gills.

Circulation and excretion
The circulatory apparatus is closely connected to the structure and development of the respiratory apparatus, although its organization differs before and after metamorphosis. In larvae this organization is similar to that of fishes, but in adults it becomes more complex and tends to resemble that found in reptiles (the creatures which follow the amphibians on the evolutionary ladder).

In larvae, the circulation is simple and complete, with a heart which has just two cavities and is washed through by venous blood. The venous sinus, which is in direct contact with the heart, sends the blood into the atrium. From here the blood passes in to the ventricle which pumps it into the gills where oxygenation takes place. At this point the blood is ready to be sent back into circulation again. During the process of metamorphosis one can observe the appearance of a septum which separates the atrium into two cavities: venous blood flows to the right-hand cavity, and arterial blood flows to the left-hand cavity, returning from the gills, and being recirculated from the heart. The ventricle, however, remains undivided.

In adults, when metamorphosis is over, the interatrial septum is completed. There is now double and complete circulation. This means there is a minor circulation (from

▼ Development of the larva of *Rana pipiens*

▼ Common toad *Bufo bufo*

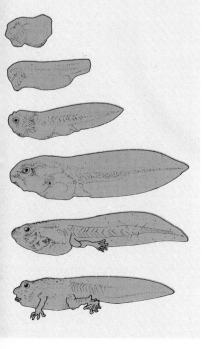

◀ Axolotls

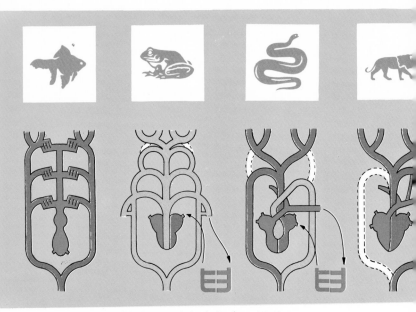

▲ Morphology of the heart and circulation in vertebrates

ventricle to lungs to left atrium) and a major circulation (from ventricle to organs and body tissues to right atrium). The ventricle is formed in such a way that it prevents the two types of blood which flow through it from mixing. The Gymnophiona and Caudata have an incomplete septum even in adults, whereas among the Anura only the Siren has a ventricular septum.

The excretory apparatus has a fairly uniform structure in all three Orders: in adults it is formed by the so-called mesonephros or primitive kidneys, elongated and flat in shape, situated at the sides of the spinal column towards its base. Each kidney is connected by a collecting tube to the urinary bladder. In male specimens the two collecting tubes, or ureters, convey both urine and the sperm produced by the testes to the cloaca; in females, however, the excretory apparatus is separate from the reproductive organs, and the ureters only convey urine. In fact the emission of a fluid from the urinary bladder of a toad is not urine but water stored in the cloaca. The cloaca is the sac into which all excretory and reproductive products pass before being discharged.

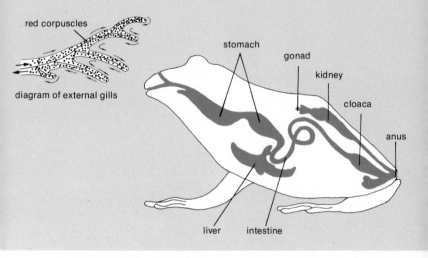

red corpuscles

diagram of external gills

stomach

gonad

kidney

cloaca

anus

liver

intestine

▲ Reproductive and excretory organs

Locomotion

The chance of survival for the amphibians in the various environments in which nature 'places' them during the different phases of their life is also conditioned by the fact that they are able to move about without difficulty, both to procure their daily food and to defend themselves from enemies or adverse climatic conditions. Amphibians are, generally speaking, aquatic animals at birth and as such move like fishes in the period of life leading to the moment of metamorphosis. When they are about a month and a half old both larvae and tadpoles swim by means of a series of accentuated contorsions of the body and their strong tail. At this stage the limbs are no more than tiny outlines of what they are to become. In the case of the Anura two months after hatching, the hind legs are completely formed but do not play any part in the movements of the body. They simply hang inertly downwards at the point where the tail itself joins the body, and the front legs are covered by the operculum. At about three months the front legs start to emerge and the tail becomes shorter until it is completely reabsorbed. The hind legs function as means of

39

support, and the animal is now practically ready to make the move to dry land. In the case of the Caudata the stages of development and the movements of the body in the larval phase are more or less similar to those of the Anura. However, the tail is bulkier and surrounded by an aquatic membrane. The order in which the limbs appear is inverted, with the front legs developing earlier than the hind ones.

Where the Gymnophiona are concerned there is just one family which leads an aquatic life as an adult as well as a larva. These are the members of the *Typhlonectidae*, found in central

▼ Marbled newt *Triturus marmoratus*

▲ Locomotion in a salamander

and southern America. These make movements in the water like those made by eels, using their laterally compressed tail. Those Caudata that are exclusively aquatic, whether subject to metamorphosis or neoteny, all have fairly small legs and a powerful tail which is often equipped with a natatory membrane or fin. The movement they make, which is also snake-like and zigzagging, is in practice carried out just by the tail. In the case of the Anura, the swimming movements are

▼ Phases in the jump of a frog

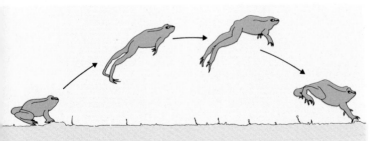

▲ Greater Siren *Siren lacertina*

made with the legs, and in particular by the hind legs which in the more aquatic species are equipped with webs between the toes. In other words, the water is pushed backwards by the hind legs with a spring-like movement, and the animal's body is thus propelled forwards.

Life on dry land involves a whole different series of requirements, the most important of which is the need to keep the body raised above the ground. However, not all the amphibians are naturally capable of doing this. As in other respects the most hampered creatures are the members of the order Gymnophiona because they have a more primitive structure. Because they are limbless, they do not walk, but instead move their snake-like bodies by slithering, using a motion like that of an earthworm. In the first phase of this motion, the head end attaches itself to the ground and drags

▲ The Clawed frog *Xenopus laevis*

▼ Hind foot of an edible frog

along the rest of the body, which grows thinner and longer; the second phase involves the rear part of the animal, which draws towards the head and in so doing causes the body to shorten and broaden.

The terrestrial Caudata have a lighter body structure than their aquatic colleagues. Although they have limbs these are not capable of keeping the body raised above the ground, and instead it is dragged along. In particular the need to make an opening in the surrounding vegetation covering the ground has given an advantage to the more slender and thinner species, which can dart like lizards with movements consisting of lateral undulations.

Among the terrestrial Anura the principal movement is the jump. The main instruments for jumping are the powerful extensor muscles in the hind legs. The function of the front legs is to act as shock-absorbers and provide a soft landing for the animal. Of all the Anura, the Ranidae are the undisputed long-jump champions: the bull-frog (*Rana catesbeiana*) makes jumps nine times the length of its body; the leopard-frog can jump 13 times the length of its body, and the semi-aquatic frog (*Acris gryllus*) can jump more than 36 times the length of its body!

The nocturnal amphibians, the Bufonidae for example, move with small, clumsy hops, as their hind legs are very short.

Among both the Anura and the Caudata there are some animals which are very well equipped for an arboreal life. Whereas the latter use their tails for climbing, using them as something of a supporting pole (this is how the tree dwelling salamander and the Sardinian salamander, *Hydromantes genei*, move about), the former use special devices on the toes of their feet. These devices are discs, or adhesive pads, (the adhesion being produced by sticky substances), and additional grip on supporting structures is given by the existence, at the skeletal level, of a supernumerary extra-phalanx. Some Hylidae and Rhacophoridae (for example New World *Phyllomedusa* and African *Chiromantis*), are characterized by a feature which is unique in the entire class: opposable thumbs on their front limbs. As a result they can move like acrobats in the branches of trees.

Continuing with the presence of specific features, we should mention the 'spades', such as horny, half-moon-shaped swellings on the hind legs of the Pelobatidae, or the curved and pointed spurs of toads. These are used for digging in the ground and also for making quick escapes by burrowing into the ground in the event of danger.

Relations with the outside world

In the larvae the eyes are like those of fishes but in adult specimens the structure of the eyes is more complex. There is development of eyelids; the lachrymal glands appear, and the eye, when static, is capable of seeing long distances. In particular, the Gymnophiona have atrophic eyes which are often covered by a layer of skin or even in some cases by bone, because the animal leads a subterranean existence. The Caudata have a fairly wide range of alternatives, depending on the environment and the lifestyle. For example: atrophied eyes occur in animals which live underground or in caves; in the aquatic forms eyes occur without eyelids; and large bulbous eyes occur in the terrestrial forms. The Anura have large eyes of varying shapes which generally protrude to give better all-round vision, which compensates for the fact that they are unable to swivel their heads.

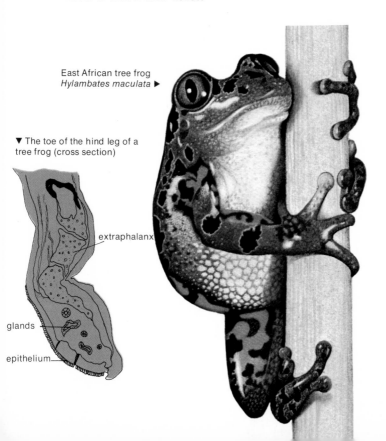

East African tree frog
Hylambates maculata ▶

▼ The toe of the hind leg of a tree frog (cross section)

extraphalanx

glands

epithelium

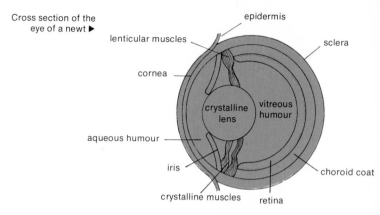

Cross section of the eye of a newt ▶

epidermis

lenticular muscles

sclera

cornea

crystalline lens

vitreous humour

aqueous humour

iris

choroid coat

crystalline muscles

retina

▼ Edible frog *Rana esculenta*

Larval amphibians and aquatic adult salamanders and Anurans, have a lateral line, consisting of a series of sense organs formed by papillae arranged symmetrically on the head and the sides of the head. The function of these is to receive the vibrations present in the water, and thus enable the animal to orient itself and find food. It would seem that the larvae of the Hynobiidae possess this sensory capacity in their mandibles, which they keep resting on the bottom.

In adults the labyrinth which forms the internal ear is coupled with the middle ear, which is formed by the eardrum. The eardrum communicates with the pharynx by means of the Eustachian tube, and in many Anura the eardrum membrane is superficial and clearly visible.

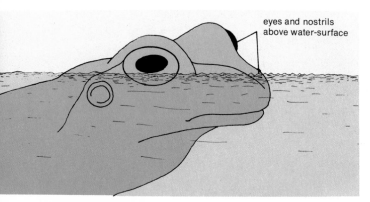

eyes and nostrils above water-surface

▲ Head of a frog partly submerged

The sense of smell aids the location of food and is localized in the epithelium of the nasal fossae. It may be enhanced by a sense organ called Jacobson's organ which consists of a pair of sacs that connects with the nasal septum and is innervated by a branch of the olfactory nerve.

The survival of the species
The first step is invariably the conquest of the female. With the exception of the Gymnophiona, whose sexual and other habits are little known (if one excludes the fact that they are the only amphibians in which internal fertilization occurs by means of an actual protrusible copulatory organ formed by the end part

47

of the cloaca), in the two other Orders we find a whole series of preliminary activities. The main purpose of these activities is to enable the two sexes to identify each other.

During this period the males of most species belonging to the Caudata engage in complicated rituals consisting of aquatic dances (many land-dwelling Caudata return to the water in these periods of their life). These dances are designed to provoke in the females the urge to gather up the spermatophores and bring them up to their cloaca, where fertilization takes place. These nuptial ceremonies are accompanied by the display of the so-called nuptial livery whereby the caudal membrane and the dorsal crest of the males grow larger, become frayed and take on splendid colours which contrast sharply with the colours of the body. Very frequently during the courtship dances special glands, which only exist in males in this phase of their existence, emit

▼ Cranium of the American Bullfrog (*Rana catesbeiana*) at the beginning of, during and at the completion of metamorphosis

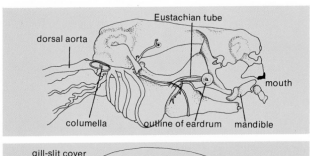

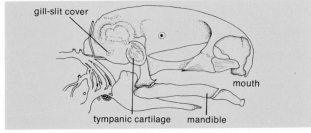

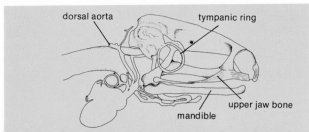

substances capable of sexually stimulating the females.
Fertilization is therefore usually internal, although there is no
actual copulation except in the case of the Sardinian newts
(*Euproctus platycephalus*) belonging to the Salamandridae,
which occur in the mountainous regions of Sardinia. Here too
reproduction occurs in the water, but the male performs no
particular ritual and by using his tail and the spurs on his hind
legs, simply fertilizes the female once he has immobilized her,
depositing the spermatophores directly in her cloaca.

In the case of the Anura, fertilization is usually external.
Male meets female in the water where increasing numbers of
each species converge at the right moment as if summoned by
some infallible instinct. Having conquered a female, often by
means of sometimes quite melodious songs (such as the very
gentle call of the midwife toad) and rather timid advances, the
male usually 'embraces' his mate by gripping her tightly

▼ Inflated vocal sac of male Sedge frog, genus *Hyperolius*

beneath the arm-pits or round the loins aided by the special devices on the front legs. This embrace is called amplexus and can be either lumbar or axillary. The duration and type of amplexus depends on the species but is only broken off when all the eggs carried by the female in her oviduct have been laid and at the same time sprayed by the male's sperm. In this Order there is one case of internal fertilization with copulation. This occurs with the tailed frog which uses the hindmost appendage of its body to introduce its sperm directly into the cloaca of the female. Internal fertilization also occurs in a few other Anura, such as the African viviparous toads and a New World leptodactylid, but in these species transfer of sperm is carried out by apposition of the cloacas.

The average number of eggs laid by the female usually runs into hundreds. This large quantity guarantees the continuity of the species, and takes into account both adverse climatic conditions and natural threats (such as parasites and predators). The Cuban *Sminthillus* is the least prolific of all the amphibians. Because of its tiny size (12 mm) the female can not accommodate more than one egg in her abdomen. At the other end of the scale, some toads of the genus *Bufo* produce about 35,000 eggs in a season. The eggs contain a fair amount of reserve matter, and are laid in chains, piles or small clusters

▼ Male Midwife toad clasps female
in lumbar amplexus

which are always wrapped in semi-transparent mucilage. This protects them from attack by other creatures, fastens them to aquatic vegetation, prevents dehydration and thus enables the embryo to develop fully.

The egg consists of a small sphere of semi-liquid protoplasm surrounded by a thick, black membrane. It contains a nucleus and in the lower part of the protoplasm, the yolk, which is the food for the new animal's early stages of life. After a period ranging from just 24 hours (as in the case of the Uruguayan *Melanophryniscus stelzneri*) to several weeks (five, eight and even twelve in the case of certain Caudata), the extremely energetic larvae eventually emerge from the eggs.

Forms of viviparity (the embryo developing inside the body of the parent) occur, although comparatively rarely, in all three Orders of the Amphibia. The spotted (or fire) salamander (*Salamandra salamandra*), for example, lays several dozen young larvae in flowing water. These larvae develop in its body during the period of winter dormancy (fertilization having occurred during the previous summer or autumn at the very latest); the Alpine (or black) salamander (*Salamandra atra*) has to live in mountains where there is insufficient water warm enough to enable the larvae to develop from eggs. It, therefore, lays a single small youngster, which the parent has developed

▼ Pair of Common toads in axillary amplexus

◀ Female salamander
(*Ambystoma maculatum*)
laying eggs

▼ Eggs of the common
toad *Bufo bufo*

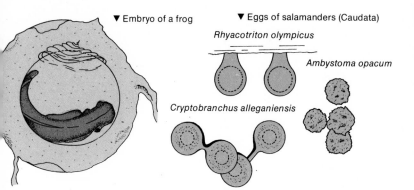

▼ Embryo of a frog   ▼ Eggs of salamanders (Caudata)

Rhyacotriton olympicus

Ambystoma opacum

Cryptobranchus alleganiensis

in its own body for a period of two to three years and which is identical to the adult and capable of living on dry land.

In the case of the Anura the only example of true viviparity occurs in the Bufonidae: the African *Nectophrynoides*. Although the male has no copulatory organ, fertilization is internal as has already been mentioned. In the body of the mother 7–14 embryos are developed, and these produce the larvae which are gill-less, tooth-less and beak-less. However, they do have a strongly vascularized tail which probably helps the gaseous and nutritive interchanges between the embryo and the walls of the uterus. At the end of the period of 'gestation' the mother gives birth to perfectly formed miniatures of the adult. True viviparity, in which the embryo is nourished by the maternal tissues, seems to be confined to *Nectophrynoides*. Ovoviviparity, however, is less unusual among the Anura and the embryos of such species as *Elentherodactylus jasperi* of Puerto Rico develop in the mother's body by subsisting on the egg yolk.

From egg to adult
Shortly after fertilization the nucleus of the egg divides into two smaller nuclei which become separate. The protoplasm also subsequently divides into two smaller masses which gather around the two nuclei and give rise to two new complete cells. The divisions of the nuclei and their respective protoplasms now occur at a fairly constant rate, until the original 'egg' becomes a kind of hollow ball covered with cells. During this process of segmentation the dimensions of the egg do not change very much, but there is a change in the overall number of cells, each with its respective nucleus and protoplasm. All this takes place in the first two or three days, after which the

53

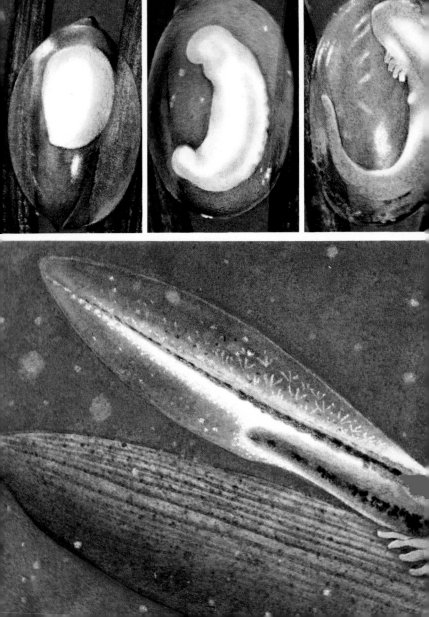

▼ Initial stages of the metamorphosis of a crested newt

sphere starts to grow longer and it is possible to make out a head and a tail inside it. The other cells of the embryo are in turn organized to form the first organs of the larva. After ten days the gelatine or jelly which still surrounds the embryo dissolves and allows the new animal to emerge into the water.

At this point the process starts to differ, depending on whether the eggs have been laid by Caudata or Anura.

In the first instance the larvae are thin and slender and on being hatched have their skeleton gills, their eyes and two sorts of small tubes which are used as anchoring organs. Rapidly the gills develop completely, the body acquires a dorsal crest and the tail acquires web-like membranes which give the animal great mobility. As far as the limbs are concerned, the front legs develop before the hind legs. The mouth, which already sports small teeth similar to adult teeth, starts supplying the larva with its first animal prey. From this stage of life onwards the Caudata are carnivorous. Further changes affecting the various organs then complete the transition from the aquatic existence to the land-based existence of the adult.

The metamorphosis of the Anura is somewhat more complex. Immediately after emerging from their eggs, the tadpoles are inactive. Up to two days before being hatched, they have no mouth or eyes. There is just one adhesive ventral organ which enables these tiny creatures to attach themselves to underwater plants. The external gills do not function. After about three days the mouth opens, the external gills receive blood, and this makes respiration possible. The tail acquires two membranes which considerably increase the creature's motor capacities. At about the three-week stage the external gills have disappeared and been replaced by internal gills. The size of the body increases and the tadpole can make nimble swimming motions in the water as it goes in search of food. Unlike the larvae of Caudata, these tadpoles are herbivorous. The small teeth and the beak with which their mouth is equipped are used to rasp the aquatic vegetation around them, which is their favourite diet. At about eight weeks the hind legs, already visible in outline at the beginning of their active life, become completely developed, and the tail begins to reduce. In many instances the tadpole rises to the surface of the water to fill up its tiny, rudimentary lungs (which are in the process of forming) with air. It takes another two or three weeks before the first front leg makes its appearance. It emerges from the spiracle, which forms the channel along which the water sucked in by the mouth flows out to wash the gills and thus provide oxygenation. Then it is the turn of the other front leg (usually the right one) to emerge, which it does by breaking the operculum (or gill cover), which is the fold of skin protecting the gills. The tail has by now become a short stump, which is soon completely re-absorbed. The young frog is now ready to leave the confines of the pond and breathe in atmospheric oxygen with its new lungs. Metamorphosis has naturally also modified the circulatory and digestive organs in respect of life on *terra firma.*

This description of the process of metamorphosis applies to the edible frog (*Rana esculenta*) which is common in Europe. Even though the duration of the various phases is approximate the patterns according to which they occur are nevertheless similiar to those of any other Anuran.

Sexual maturity is reached in a second stage. The common frog is capable of procreating four years after metamorphosis has taken place. Other species are considerably more precocious or slow-developing and this is probably closely connected with their environment.

Some amphibians keep their larval characteristics into their adult stage. For example the axolotl, the larval form of the Mexican Salamander, may remain in this *neotenic* form indefinately even though it has become sexually mature.

▼ Adult and neotenic forms of Mexican salamander *Ambystoma mexicanum* (see page 16)

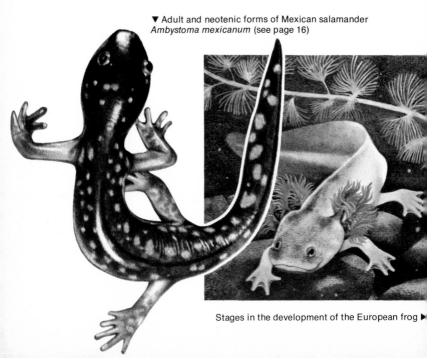

Stages in the development of the European frog ▶

Behaviour

'Behaviour' can be defined as the method of swimming or jumping, creeping or climbing; the movements made when eating, mating, breathing, or trying to attract the attention of a mate (male or female) of the same species. However, 'behaviour' does not stop here, as it also embraces the ability to emit 'intentional' sounds or make certain body-movements to communicate to others the attainment of sexual maturity.

Many amphibians change the colour of their skin; others cover themselves with sticky secretions; others still assume terrifying attitudes to show either their fear or courage in the face of a foe.

All these signs, which vary from species to species, are repeated within the same species from one generation to the next, being based on a pre-established code.

Courtship displays

In an earlier chapter we saw how the need to guarantee the continuity of the species has produced a number of different courtship displays which occur at the beginning of the mating season. The main purpose of this behaviour is to prevent the occurrence of random mating between different species which could result in irregular features. These displays involve the appearance of secondary sexual features, which only last for the duration of the reproductive period. In the Caudata the main features are bright and showy colours, crests and brightly-coloured membranes on the back and tail, the swelling up of the male cloaca from which the spermatophores, are produced and, unique among the Order, the caudal spur of the Caucasian salamander.

▲ A pair of crested newts *Triturus cristatus*

In the Anura, it is the voice which plays the major rôle. In those species equipped with a voice the male has a typical sexual call, which is the only call to which females of the same species will respond to. This call is often amplified by the sound-boxes formed by the vocal sacs which also vary in shape, size and position in the various members of the Orders. Other identification factors are all the cutaneous formations, such as dermal spines, and thumb and chest pads which enable the male to grasp the female more tightly during the act of mating.

On attaining sexual maturity the Anura can also change their 'livery' and the males are often strikingly different in coloration and pattern from the females.

Care of the young

Attached to some plant or stone in the water, the eggs of amphibians 'arrange' things for themselves as far as their development is concerned. The gelatine which surrounds them reduces the dangers of drying or the threat of attack from other creatures. Parents protect their young and ensure their survival by building well constructed nests, or even carrying all their offspring round with them until they have grown enough and become sufficiently independent. Among the Anura the

▲ A pair of West African frogs *Hylarana albolabris*

commonest nests are those made of foam which are built by certain tropical tree-frogs, probably to prevent the heat from drying up the brood. Once the appropriate place has been chosen, in the shelter of a leaf of some aquatic plant, the female starts to lay her eggs which the male immediately fertilizes. As the eggs gradually emerge from the cloaca, the mucous secretion which accompanies this act is 'beaten' by the hind legs of both parents until a thick foam, which is light in texture, has been produced. The female then carefully presses leaves over the small mass of foam to make the nest stronger. After this the parents move off. In the meantime the eggs start to develop and part of the foam of the nest dissolves, thus creating within it a kind of tiny aquarium where the newborn tadpoles can live.

A more refined nest-building technique is that used by the blacksmith frog (*Hyla faber*) found in Argentina and Brazil. These frogs usually live in trees, but during the mating season return to the water. Choosing shallow, calm water, the males build a crater-like nest of mud, in which a pool forms. When the nest is completed, the male sits in the middle of it and summons a female so he can fertilize her eggs. When fertilization has occurred, the parents leave the nest in which the tadpoles can develop.

One of the most original nests is that made by the male vaquero (*Rhinoderma darwini*) found in Chile and on the borders of Argentina. As soon as it is possible to glimpse the embryos born inside the large eggs laid by the female, males gather up clusters of them with their tongues and slip them inside their very large vocal sacs. In the strange 'nursery' the young tadpoles complete their development, eating their own yolk and breathing by means of their large vascularized tails.

Apart from the construction of nests, certain Anura use even more 'personal' systems of incubation and care of their young. In the case of the genus *Dendrobates* the eggs are laid on the male's back, attached to the skin, and hatch here without any water save the occasional shower. A unique form of parental care occurs in the South American frogs of the genus *Pipa* (family Pipidae). The amplectic pair indulge in a series of somersaults in water, the female laying eggs while in the middle of one somersault. As the eggs are passed out they are fertilized by the male and drop on to his belly but as the pair flip over and head down through the water the eggs roll over the female's back and settle in pockets in her skin. The closely pressed body of the male prevents the eggs from falling off. When the operation has been successfully completed, and sixty or so eggs have been loaded on to the mother's back, the father departs. Meanwhile the skin on the female's back has swollen and envelops each of the eggs in its own separate cell. Here each egg will complete its development until such time as the perfectly formed baby frogs are strong enough to break through the cell-walls and come out into the open.

Where the Discoglossidae are concerned, it is the father who takes charge of the eggs. He carries them around with him, until they hatch, wrapped around his hind legs. The incubation period is roughly three weeks, and the tadpoles hatch into water, the father having made sure he is in water when he feels the moment of hatching is imminent.

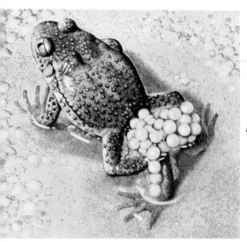

▲ Midwife toad *Alytes obstetricans*

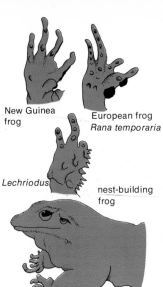

New Guinea frog

European frog *Rana temporaria*

Lechriodus

nest-building frog

▲ Cutaneous spines

Nest of African grey tree frog *Chiromantis petersi kelleri* ▶

▲ Nuptial pads of male hairy frog

The social life of amphibians

Amphibians are somewhat hallmarked by the absence of specifically organized or significant forms of social life which is in contrast to other classes of vertebrates.

At the larval level there is a tendency towards gregariousness in the tadpoles of certain spadefoot toads (Pelobatidae); when an adverse situation occurs they group together to form a thick swarm. This then sinks to the bottom of the pond and they try to shift the debris that has collected there by all flapping their long tails in unison. Their behaviour is similar when the water-level drops. In such cases they all work together to hollow out tiny cavities in the bottom of the pond with the purpose of collecting the remaining water in a smaller area than the pond itself, to stop it evaporating too quickly.

Similarly the tadpoles of another spadefoot toad, Hurter's spadefoot toad, show a tendency to group together when they have to leave the pond for the first time. As if driven by some common instinct they all gather together under cover of night and make their way in their thousands on to the bank.

Among the Caudata there are not many instances of

▼ A pond containing edible frogs

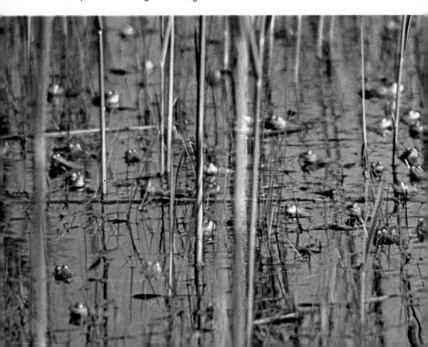

gregariousness either during the larval stage or as adults. In certain species life is hallmarked by forms of isolation interrupted only by mating. The only species which apparently enjoys company is the spotted salamander (*Salamandra salamandra*), which is quite common in Europe. Often, several adults will seek a common hideout, which sometimes causes widescale deaths from 'salamander disease' (or plague). This serious disease is very infectious and is caused by a fungus. It can pass through such 'colonies' and totally wipe out the population. In temperate regions toads, frogs and tree-frogs go in search of company on only two occasions during their life. Firstly during the mating season and secondly when, with the first frost or dry spell, they abandon all other activities and enter the long period of hibernation (or aestivation).

In the first case it is mainly the males which gather together, forming 'choirs', to invite the females to be their mates. These assemblies usually take place at night and the male's voice helps identify his sex and his species, and is the principal mechanism for preventing cross mating. In the second case, the tendency to associate can be interpreted as an instinctive drive to cope with unfavourable living conditions.

▼ The edible frog *Rana esculenta*

Attack and defence

Individual survival depends on the tactics and mechanisms employed for hunting and defence. With the exception of just two species of salamandrids (*Pleurodeles waltl*, found in the Iberian peninsula and Morocco, and *Tylotriton verrucosus* which ranges from India to China), which have a series of spines along their backs, the Caudata are without any specific defence organs. As a result they entrust their safety to fleeing from the enemy, and hiding from him. For these creatures coloration of the skin is the fundamental and most important means of defence, and it is rare for them to be taken unawares by danger. Moving at great speed, and with their extraordinary sense of direction and orientation, they manage to keep the aggressor at a distance and at the same time, as a result of hormonal and physical stimuli, their skin changes colour and blends with the terrain around them. As well as the device of mimetism or camouflage, the Caudata are capable of increasing the sticky and irritant secretions produced by their skin glands. They can also 'feign death' to distract the enemy's attention, and assume a frightening appearance by, for

▼ Female Pyrenean newt (*Euproctus asper*) feigning death

Horned frog
Ceratophyrs ornata ▶

example, displaying their belly which is brightly and perhaps surprisingly coloured. The three-toed amphiuma (*Amphiuma tridactylum*) has more active defence mechanisms, biting its foes with its sharp, pointed teeth, as does *Hemidactylium scutatum*. The latter belongs to the Plethodontidae, which, like certain salamanders, snaps off its own tail to distract its enemy. The Anura have similar defence tactics, but are also often equipped with actual weapons such as teeth and spines.

▼ Common toad *Bufo bufo*

Ecology

Where amphibians live

A basic fact has emerged from the brief review so far presented of amphibians and their activities. This is that these creatures still show remarkable adaptability to any and every environment, just as they displayed this same capacity when they made their first appearance on the Earth.

The most interesting feature of this class with regard to its relationship with the world about it is that on the whole its

members have an aversion to salt water. There are, however, a variety of amphibians which are known to tolerate brackish conditions. For example, *Bufo arenarum* of Argentina lives in brackish pools along the coastline, while *Bufo halophilus*, found in Nevada and California, lives in salt and alkaline water, and *Rana cancrivora* of S.E. Asia eats crabs and can survive in sea water.

We have also seen how, for these creatures, the limiting

factor is an adequate percentage of humidity. The layer of fluid which keeps their skin constantly moist in fact ensures cutaneous respiration, which complements and supplements pulmonary breathing. Many amphibians have nocturnal habits. During the daylight hours they hide in the ground or in sand where the ambient temperature is lower and where, as a result, they can always find a certain amount of humidity. In Europe, for example, one may find salamanders at night or after a heavy shower, but they are certainly never to be found at the hottest time of day. Where frogs are concerned, the edible frog (*Rana esculenta*) which lives by small ponds alternates brief hunting forays on dry land with similarly brief periods spent in the water. The common European frog (*Rana temporaria*) on the other hand can often be seen on *terra firma* in spring and autumn, or even in summer after a shower of rain, but you will not come across it on sunny days.

In regions with a temperate or temperate-to-cold climate, amphibians spend the winter months buried in the ground or in sand, or in cracks in rocks, or, in some cases, in the mud at the bottom of ponds and pools. This period of inactivity, called hibernation, coincides with the length of the cold season of the year. In tropical zones, hibernation is replaced (and only in exceptional cases complemented) by aestivation. This is also a form of deceleration of the metabolism, the aim of which is primarily to relieve the animal from the effects of excessive heat and drought.

Today, amphibians are to be found in every continent except Antarctica. The tropical regions have the greatest variety of species, ranging from forms which have totally adapted to living in trees (even the eggs and tadpoles are respectively laid and developed in rainwater caught by leaves) to the world of jumping and burrowing amphibians, slow and sluggish creatures which live at the foot of these same trees. Deserts also offer refuge and food to certain members of this class, which manage to find water by digging long tunnels in the arid land. As far as latitude and altitude are concerned, amphibians can still survive in regions where the climatic conditions would not seem to comply with their requirements. Thus, *Bufo boreas* occurs in the Yukon range of mountains in southern Alaska and *Rana cantabrigensis* occurs in both Alaska and Canada. Also, north of the Arctic Circle one finds the common European frog, *Rana temporaria*, the wood frog *Rana sylvatica* in Alaska and *Hynobius keyserlingi*, a small hynobiid member of the Caudata which quite happily tolerate temperatures below freezing point. The adaptations which enable these

species and a few others to live in such intensely cold conditions are, first and foremost, a speeding-up of the processes of development from the egg the larval and finally the adult stage. They also possess the ability to prolong the period of hibernation and (this feature only applies to the Hynobiidae) the capacity, as the cold season approaches, to get rid of the body fluid so as to increase the saline concentration in the organism, and thus reduce the risk of freezing to death.

Although they are numerically scarce, there are nevertheless certain species which live at very high altitudes. In Italy, the Alpine or black salamander (*Salamandra atra*) is found at altitudes of 3000 m. The European frog, which is also very common in cool, hilly regions, can be found even above the 3000 metre mark in mountain pastures, by small watering-places used by livestock. The record distribution in terms of altitude would nevertheless seem to be held by the green toad (*Bufo viridis*) which is to be found at sea-level in Europe and at 4560 metres in the Himalayas.

Amphibians do not venture very far underground because their soft bodies are not capable of supporting the weight of a large mass of earth. As a result they rarely penetrate more than a few inches or so below ground-level, although the Australian water-holding frogs can, in suitable soil, excavate long tunnels, and other species may venture a little further when in rock crevices and caves.

The world's amphibians

The Caudata of the Palearctic Region (Europe, Africa north of Sahara, Asia north of the Himalayas), comprise the Hynobiidae, Salamandridae, Plethodontidae, Cryptobranchidae and the Proteidae with just one species, the olm (*Proteus anguineus*). The Anura are represented by the families Ranidae and Bufonidae, as well as the Hylidae, Pelobatidae and Discoglossidae.

Within the Nearctic Region (North America to northern Mexico), the Caudata include a few salamandrids, numerous plethodontids, as well as Ambystomatidae, Sirenidae and Amphiumidae, Proteidae and Cryptobranchidae. The Anura are represented by a large number of Ranidae, Bufonidae and Hylidae.

Within the Ethiopian Region (Africa south of the Sahara and southern Arabia), there are no Caudata at all, and where the Anura are concerned the tree-frogs are replaced by the Rhacophoridae and Hyperoliidae. There are, however, large numbers of Ranidae, Bufonidae and Microhylidae as well as

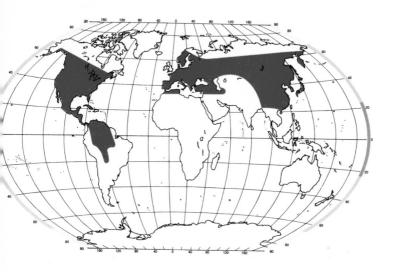

▲ Major areas of distribution of Caudata

certain members of the family Pipidae. This zone, which resembles the tropical regions quite closely, also contains certain Gymnophiona.

Within the Malagasy Region (Madagascar and other nearby islands) there are no Caudata and, among the Anura, no Bufonidae or Pipidae. Only a few species of Ranidae are found here. There are many Rhacophoridae and Microhylidae.

Within the Oriental Region (Asia south of the Himalayas, the Philippines and Malaysia) where the Anura are concerned, the Ranidae, Rhacophoridae, Microhylidae, Bufonidae and Pelobatidae are the main families. There are no Pipidae, but there are Gymnophiona.

The Neotropical Region (from Mexico to South America) contains many Hylidae, Bufonidae, Leptodactylidae, Pipidae, Ranidae and Microhylidae as well as other smaller families. Caudata are represented by a rich variety of Plethodontidae. The majority of Gymnophiona occur in this region.

Within the Australian Region (Oceania) there are no Rhacophoridae, very few Microhylidae and Ranidae, and plenty of tree frogs (Pelodryadae) and Leptodactylidae. The only Bufonidae is the introduced Marine Toad (*Bufo marinus*).

73

74

◀ Leopard frog
Rana pipiens

Amphibians and man

It has already been mentioned earlier how, in byegone days, amphibians were associated with the world of witchcraft and magic. These traditions which are still being carried on today by certain primitive peoples. From the nutritional viewpoint, they have always been considered a delicacy by gourmets, rather than a major source of food.

In the Far East, the giant Japanese and Chinese salamanders are still sought after for their flesh which is apparently very delicate. In the American continent, and in Mexico in particular, there is a marked preference for the axolotl, the neotenic form of *Ambystoma mexicanum*, the Mexican salamander.

In Europe only the Anura are considered suitable for human consumption. Although the flesh of a frog has a fairly high protein content, comparable to that of chicken meat, and is thus easily digestible and easy to assimilate, their rather slow rate of development (a frog takes about four years to reach a weight and size enough to tempt the gourmet) has meant that the idea of raising frogs has never become very successful.

Apart from the food value the importance of frogs and of amphibians belonging to the genus *Xenopus* resides in the fact that these creatures are often used in the laboratory for various types of experiment. These range from those to do with organ transplants, to tests to ascertain the state of pregnancy in women, to techniques developed to extract from the poisonous species certain alkaloids for use in pharmaceutics.

Finally, mention should be made of *Rana catesbeiana*, the bull frog which is very common in America and is raised in certain European countries for competitive purposes. These frogs are taught to compete in jumping races and at Calaveras, in California, there is an annual and authentic frogs' meeting.

▼ Common Spadefoot toad
Pelobates fuscus

Classification

There are about 2400 species of amphibians living on our planet which have been divided into three Orders, on the basis of their morphological, anatomical and physiological features. Listed here are the various families belonging to the three orders of Gymnophiona, Caudata and Anura.

Gymnophiona
Family Caeciliidae: Central and South America, Asia, Africa and the Seychelles. All caecilians are limbless and worm-like in appearance and have a tentacle in front of the eye. Some have scales embedded in the skin. The tongue is fastened and capable of only limited movement. Eyes may be visible, indistinct or covered by bone. They all have internal fertilization, are oviparous or ovoviviparous. Terrestrial.
Family Ichthyophidae: Asia and S. America. Terrestrial.
Family Typhlonectidae: South America. Aquatic.
Family Scolecomorphidae: Africa. Terrestrial.

Caudata
Family Hynobiidae: consists of 30 species widespread in Asia, and Japan, these are regarded as the most primitive.
Family Cryptobranchidae: consists of three species of enormous dimensions. The Cryptobranchidae are always aquatic.
Family Sirenidae: occupied a dubious systematic position until a few years ago. They have primitive features and the body is worm-like. They are perennibranchiate (gills persist throughout life) and always aquatic. There are only three known living species, all in America. Fertilization is external.

Family Proteidae: consists of six species, one of which is European, the others American. All the forms are neotenic.

Family Amblystomatidae: consists of 32 species, all found in North America and Mexico. Some are optionally neotenic.

Family Salamandridae: A widespread family containing all the typical salamanders and newts, it occurs in Europe, Asia, Japan, North and Central America and North Africa. The eyes have eyelids. Adults usually spend most of their lives on land.

Family Amphiumidae: consists of only three species, and they occur in the south eastern region of the United States. The amphiuma has a long body with small and useless legs, a smooth skin, aquatic habits, and no eyelids.

Family Plethodontidae: contains 183 species in North, Central and South America and Southern Europe. They have penetrated a wide variety of habitats: terrestrial, arboreal, aquatic and cavernicolous and some are even burrowers. None of the Plethodontidae has lungs. Two species are neotenic.

Anura

Family Ascaphidae: includes the only anura with amphicoelous vertebrae. No tail, but caudal muscles in the one American genus. These frogs live in New Zealand and in the northwestern region of the United States.

Family Pipidae: includes fairly primitive aquatic frogs, with opisthocoelous vertebrae and no tongue. They live in Africa, south of the Sahara and southern America.

Family Discoglossidae: consists of toads living in Europe, N.W. Africa, Asia and the Philippines. As adults they have ribs, a primitive feature.

Family Pelobatidae: includes species of frogs which are very common in Europe, North Africa, S.E. Asia and North America. Many of them are burrowers. Generally nocturnal, some forms live by day buried in the ground.

Family Bufonidae: includes a large number of species some of which attain a considerable size. They have adapted to life on dry land even when there is little humidity. Found on all major land masses of the world, except New Guinea, New Zealand, and Madagascar. The family includes the strikingly coloured *Atelopus* found in Central and South America.

Family Hylidae: predominantly a New World family of tree frogs and containing the Marsupial frogs and some other egg-carrying species. Terminal phalanx in each toe is claw-shaped. Intercalary element in the toe short, disc-like and cartilaginous. Tarsal bones separated. Includes a few forms capable of parachuting (*Agalychnis*).

Family Leptodactylidae: a large family of frogs from South America and the Australian Papuan region. Only one genus occurs elsewhere (S. Africa); terrestrial and aquatic forms.

Family Dehdrobatidae: includes a fair number of nimble creatures with bright colours and sometimes tiny dimensions; often with strong cutaneous poison.

Family Ranidae: consists of a very large number of species found all over the world. They have a streamlined shape suited to jumping, pointed face and large eyes.

Family Rhacophoridae: a large group of mainly arboreal forms found chiefly in S.E. Asia and Madagascar with one genus in Africa. Superficially resemble the Hylidae and like them have intercalary cartilages in the digits. Pupil horizontal. Contains foam nest builders and 'flying' frogs.

Family Microhylidae: a widely distributed family of terrestrial and arboreal frogs in Old and New World tropics.

Family Phrynomeridae: includes only small frogs of the genus *Phrynomerus* found in Africa south of the Sahara. Terrestrial; skin secretes toxic substances.

Family Hyperoliidae: a large group of largely African arboreal frogs including the gaily coloured sedge frogs. Adhesive discs and intercalary cartilages present. Pupil vertical or horizontal.

Family Rhinophrynidae: includes only the Mexican burrowing frog. It is tooth-less and its tongue is unattached in front. It has a huge shovel on its hind foot that enables it to burrow well.

Family Brachycephalidae: includes only the tiny Brazilian, golden frog which has a bony plate fused to its backbone.

Family Centrolenidae: a small group of New World arboreal

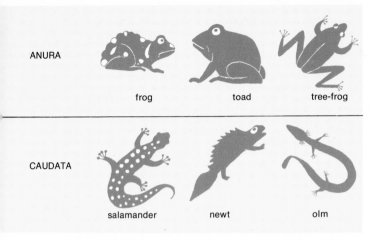

ANURA — frog, toad, tree-frog

CAUDATA — salamander, newt, olm

frogs. Most members are small and coloured green.
Family Pseudidae: a South American group of aquatic frogs
containing the Paradoxical frog with the enormous tadpole.
Thumb opposable. Tarsal bones separated. Long bony
intercalary element provides an extra phalanx in each toe.
Family Pelodryadidae: Australasian tree frogs previously
partitioned in the Hylidae, differing from that family in throat
musculature. The familial status is questionable.

Class	Subclass	Order	Suborder
Amphibia	Labyrinthodontia	Temnospondyli	Rhachitomi Stereospondyli Plagiosauria
		Batrachosauria	Anthrocosauria Gephyrostegoidea Seymouriamorpha
		Ichthyostegalia	
	Lepospondyli	Nectridea Aistopoda Microsauria	
	Lissamphibia	Proanura Anura Caudata Gymnophiona	

Classification of fossil and modern amphibians ▲

Reptiles

Introduction

The history of this class of Vertebrates is a fascinating one. The reptiles have existed on earth for about 300 million years, during which time they have successfully adapted to many changes in climatic conditions and environment. In the early part of their history many varied species of reptiles evolved and for over 100 million years they dominated land, sea and air. About 65 million years ago, however, fauna was almost wiped out and of the sixteen orders existing in the Mesozoic Era, only four continued to flourish until the present day.

Although amphibians evolved before the reptiles, the latter group of creatures were considerably more successful, and the

key to this success was the development of the hard-shelled or amniotic egg.

The eggs of amphibians lack both an outer shell and membranes to protect the embryo. They are enclosed in their soft, gelatinous sacs, and must be deposited in a moist place to prevent desiccation. Reptilian eggs, however, are protected by a fairly tough protective shell and the embryo is surrounded by three membranes (amnion, chorion and allantois) which make the eggs relatively resistant to desiccation. The absence of the typical aquatic larval stage followed by metamorphosis was instrumental in freeing reptiles from the aquatic world.

Quite how and where this type of egg came into being for the first time is still the topic of much hypothesis and supposition even today. Some authors maintain that amniotic eggs and eggs with shells must have been laid by animals which were still aquatic and who managed in this way to protect their offspring from being attacked by possible enemies; others claim that this 'invention' might have been made by mountain-dwelling creatures, in habitats where there was a scarcity of still or slow-flowing water and where the young developed 'directly', omitting a larval stage; because external fertilization was impossible in such conditions (the fast-flowing water would have swept away the spermatozoa before they had had a chance to fertilize the eggs), a process of internal fertilization might have evolved before the formation of the shell, which would then have protected the egg when it was laid on dry land.

The name of this class refers to one of the most distinctive features of its member animals: their manner of locomotion, by creeping, crawling or slithering (Latin *repere* means 'to crawl' or 'to creep'). The reptiles, however, do not, nor did they, include only creeping animal forms, but also animals which move by using very varied types of locomotion.

This class also has other peculiar features: poikilothermism, which they share in common with amphibians: scaly skin; the presence of lungs; the presence – at least in primitive forms – of four legs (in some cases evolution has brought about the loss of two or even all four external limbs).

Today there are six groups of reptiles: the tortoises and turtles (Testudines), which include some 300 species of animals; the crocodiles, caymans, alligators and gharials (Crocodylia), of which there are 21 species; the Rhynchocephalia, with just one species, the New Zealand tuatara; the Saurians or lizards, the largest group with some 3000 species living in a very wide variety of habitats; the Amphisbaenians or Worm Lizards, a group of worm-like burrowers most of which lack limbs (fewer than 100 species are known); and the Serpentes or snakes, the only truly 'creeping' reptiles, with some 2700 species. But the importance of the reptiles does not end here: certain species in this class gave rise to the group of *Therapsida*, the forebears of the mammals, which emerged in the Triassic period 220,000,000 years ago, and others give rise to the group of *Thecodontia*, forefathers of the primitive birds, which first appeared about 150 million years ago.

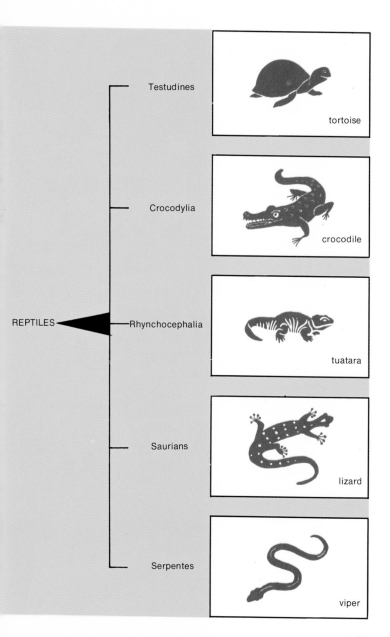

REPTILES

Testudines — tortoise

Crocodylia — crocodile

Rhynchocephalia — tuatara

Saurians — lizard

Serpentes — viper

85

INTRODUCTION

Ancient and modern reptiles can be divided into specific groups on the basis of certain cranial features:

The Anapsida, characterized by a primitive type of skull which has no aperture in the temporal region (e.g. sea turtle).

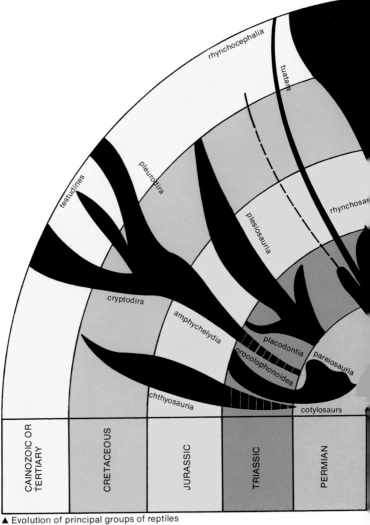

rhynchocephalia

tuatara

pleurodira

testudines

plesiosauria

rhynchosa

cryptodira

amphychelydia

placodontia

procolophonoidea

pareiosauria

chthyosauria

cotylosaurs

CAINOZOIC OR TERTIARY	CRETACEOUS	JURASSIC	TRIASSIC	PERMIAN

▲ Evolution of principal groups of reptiles

The Lepidosauria and the Archosauria, with a diapsid cranium or skull, i.e. with two temporal openings which may be bounded by bony arcades (e.g. the tuatara).

The Euryapsida, now extinct, with a single temporal fossa, corresponding to the upper fossa in the diapsid skull.

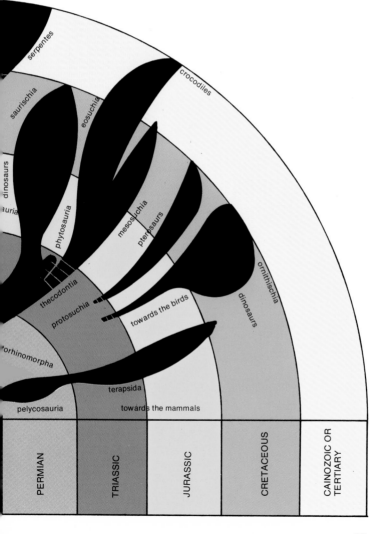

The Synapsida, with a single temporal fossa corresponding to the lower fossa of the diapsid skull.

The Anapsida, with their massive skull, include the forebears of the entire class of reptiles: the Cotylosaurs. These creatures appeared in the height of the Palaeozoic Era, as is evidenced by certain fossil remains unearthed in Carboniferous rocks; to begin with they showed a certain similarity to the amphibians (structure of the skull and dentition); at a later stage they became more specialized, assuming more powerful and better protected physique and larger dimensions, appropriate, in other words, to essentially herbivorous animals with a slow and heavy gait. The first

▼ The evolution of the dinosaurs

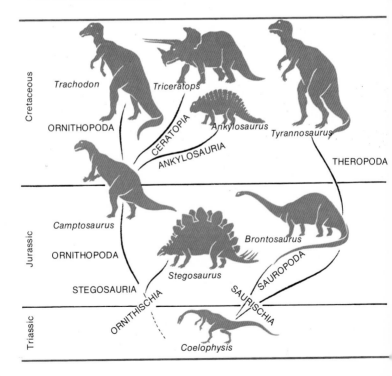

▲ Reconstruction of Pteranodontidae (*Cretaceous*)

true tortoises and turtles developed from these forms at a much later date, towards the end of the Triassic Era. During the approximately 200,000,000 years which saw the appearance, development and rise of the reptiles, many other forms emerged which were either partly or thoroughly adapted to the aquatic environment. Among these were the so-called euryapsid reptiles, which lived from the Permian Era (the period to which the genus *Araeoscelis*, an animal with a long tail not unlike present-day tropical lizards, is attributed) to the end of the Cretaceous Era, when the last marine Sauropterygia became extinct; these latter had long flexible necks designed for catching the small fishes which made up their diet, and legs transformed into paddles.

However, the Euryapsida were not the only group that included aquatic creatures. The reptiles best suited to this habitat were the Ichthyopterygia with their fish-shaped bodies; back in those days they represented the equivalent of our present-day dolphins. Ranging from a few centimetres to several metres in length, the Ichthyopterygia resembled today's sharks, with very strong tail fins, tapered skulls and the sharp teeth of carnivores.

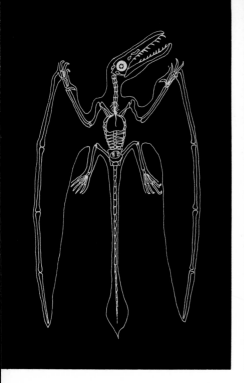

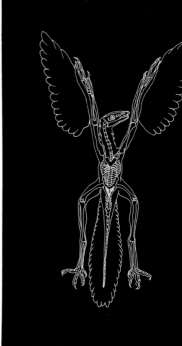

▲ *Pterosaurus*   ▲ *Archaeopteryx lithographica*

The Synapsida were typical dry-land dwellers; both carnivorous and herbivorous, they soon showed a gradual and different development in the structure of their teeth and skulls, which became remarkably compact. The most important aspect of this group, and in particular of the members of the Order Therapsida, was the series of modifications that affected the skeleton. This enabled the legs to run over hard terrain. Although numerous, varied and adapted to extremely diverse environments, Anapsida, Euryapsida and Synapsida never achieved the diversity and development of the reptiles with diapsid skulls, such as the Archosauria and the Lepidosauria. The 'flying reptiles' were also Archosauria, namely the Pterosauria (Pterodactyls), which survived until the end of the Mesozoic Era and then vanished altogether. The size of these creatures varied between that of a blackbird to that of a truly gigantic bird with a wingspan of 16 metres (as in the case of *Quetzalcoatlus*, or the somewhat smaller *Pteranodon* of

▲ South American caiman *Caiman crocodilus sclerops*
▼ Fossil head of an ichthyosaur *Ichthyosaurus longirostris*

91

▲ Ancient reptiles: (1) *Nyctosaurus* (2.40 m); (2) *Moschops* (2.40 m);
(3) *Diadectes* (1.80 m)

▼ Marine reptiles: (1) *Cryptocleidus* (3.30 m); (2) *Placodus* (2.40 m);
(3) *Kronosaurus* (12.50 m)

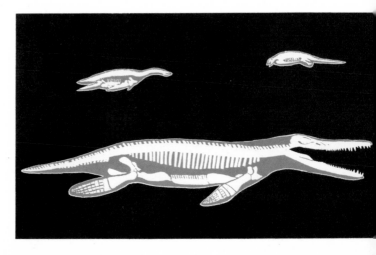

8 metres). The skull was made lighter by having apertures and pneumatic bones like present-day birds, and there were wide wing-like webs between the front and hind legs which enabled them to glide. The overlords of the fern-forests which covered the Earth throughout the Mesozoic Era were the dinosaurs, those 'fearsome reptiles' which lived unrivalled on the land for 130,000,000 years and then died out completely.

Outwardly they were all fairly similar. They had a short, strong trunk, supported by long, pillar-like legs, a small head at the end of a long neck, and a long and often tapering tail. Individually, these animals had numerous differences in size, shape and habit. There was *Brontosaurus* (25 metres long) with its broad feet, equipped with three large, hooked claws; slender *Diplodocus* with its long neck and whip-like tail; *Brachiosaurus* (22 metres long); and many more. When it came the decline of this race was rapid but although there are many hypotheses, the extinction of the dinosaurs is still an unsolved mystery.

The subclass Archosauria contained the largest number of the primitive forms but the subclass Lepidosauria consists of the most plentiful reptiles in the modern natural world. This subclass includes all those types which have their bodies covered with scales (the Greek word *lepís* means a scale).

In 1914 a small fossil reptile was discovered in Permian rocks in South Africa. This was given the name *Youngina* and is considered to be the forebear of all the Diapsida. Two different groups originated from this primitive genus: the Archosauria, which reached the highest degree of reptilian specialization during the prehistoric period (consider the extremely large number of species embraced by the Orders of thecodonts, pterosaurs and dinosaurs), and the Lepidosauria, which were possibly less varied precisely because they included the most ancient original forms. In this respect it is worth remembering that members of this group, which were adapted to a typically marine habitat, have also been found on Italian soil. One such is the *Askeptosaurus italicus.* Extremely old in origin, it seems to have lived on the shores of the sea that then covered much of present-day Lombardy. It was about 2 metres in length, slender and streamlined, with strong and very sharp teeth as befitting an aquatic, carnivorous creature. Consequently it was an animal with predatory habits. The long, tapered tail and the probably palmate or webbed feet are clear evidence of the habitat in which it lived.

▲ Emerald tree boa *Corallus caninus*

▼ Hermann's tortoise *Testudo hermanni*

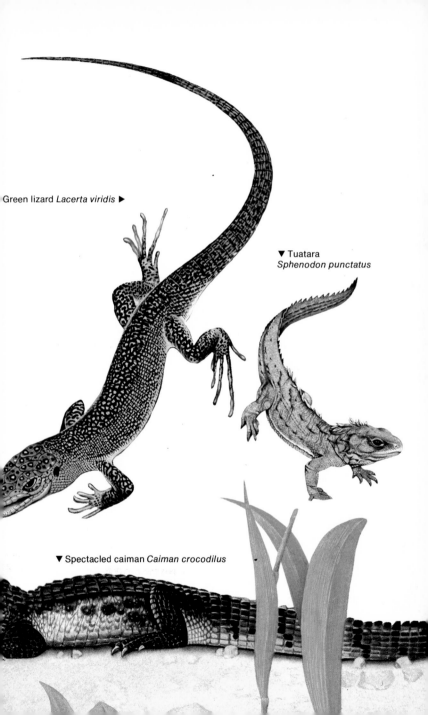

Green lizard *Lacerta viridis* ▶

▼ Tuatara
Sphenodon punctatus

▼ Spectacled caiman *Caiman crocodilus*

Structure

Shapes and sizes

In the animal world, few species are as widespread, on such a massive and vast scale, as the reptiles.

Within this one class, the first of the vertebrates to successfully liberate itself from water, one encounters a return to water. Currently existing groups of reptiles (with the exception of the Rhynchocephalia and Amphisbaenia) include both amphibious and totally aquatic forms. The only sea-snake to come ashore are those that lay eggs. All other sea snakes have developed the capacity to deliver live and perfectly formed young (viviparity) at sea.

Despite the considerable numerical reduction in their ranks, the surviving Orders of reptiles still show a wide diversity of form and habits. This is apparent from looking at these creatures' morphology.

At the beginning of the reptilian era, the tortoises and turtles were already characterized by having their body enclosed in a bony shell formed by two sections. These consisted of the dorsal section (the carapace) and the ventral section (the

plastron), joined together at the sides. From the front of this shell emerged the head, neck and front legs, and behind, the tail and the hind legs. Despite the inconvenience of having the body confined in a hard 'box' of this sort, the tortoises, terrapins and turtles have managed to adapt to life on dry land as well as life in water, be it salt or fresh water. Compared with their remote ancestors, present-day tortoises and turtles have thinner shells, and in some cases they are even soft. Thus the giant leathery sea-turtle has a non-ossified plastron, and the aptly named soft-shelled turtles (super family Trionychoidea) found in fresh water in the tropics, have a soft shell covered simply by a leathery skin with no horny plates.

In addition to the features of the shell, the legs and heads can also differ considerably. The terrestrial species have strong legs equipped with very well-developed claws, while the fresh water species have webbed feet and the marine species have flippers suitable for swimming. Some fresh water species have a kind of elongated proboscis in which the nostrils are set, so that they can continue to breathe with just the smallest part of the head protruding above the water-surface. The crocodilians (or Crocodylia) are the last survivors of the line which also gave rise to the dinosaurs, and they are the reptiles best adapted to the amphibious life. Their strong and fairly thickset bodies end in a long tail which is heavy and muscular, laterally compressed and rudder-like and helps propel the animal while it is swimming. The legs are short and the feet, although almost always webbed, are used mainly on dry land, and give the crocodilians an awkward and heavy gait. The most distinctive feature, from the morphological viewpoint, is the head, which is flattish and elongated, does not have fleshy lips, but does have sharp teeth. Nostrils and eyes and ears are situated on top of the head which enables the animal to receive all the stimuli of the outside world without leaving the water.

As far as the Rynchocephalia are concerned there is today only one creature alive which belongs to this Order, and this animal exists in just a few small islands in New Zealand. It is the so-called tuatara or *Sphenodon*. In appearance it is quite similar to a lizard as far as colour, its way of periodically changing its skin, and the dentate crest along its head and back are concerned. However, its anatomy and skeleton differs considerably from lizards. The skull has a supplementary bone which keeps the mandible fixed. There are no external ears, and there is not even a male copulatory organ. On top of the head it has the famous 'third eye' which is particularly clearly defined in young specimens, although it does not appear to have a visual function.

Although they belong to the same Order, the Squamata, the Sauria and Serpentes are considerably different. Firstly, the Serpentes usually have no legs. Thus we find apodous (legless) Saurians (the American, Asian and European glass-snakes; the slow-worms, found typically in Europe; and almost all of the burrowing amphisbaenians which occur in both the Old and New Worlds) and Serpentes with legs (the anaconda, boas, pythons and three groups of primitive burrowing snakes all have rudimentary hind legs which are generally used as stimulatory organs during mating). Another difference between the two groups is the existence, in most Saurians, of an external ear which all snakes lack. Furthermore in the latter the middle ear is also absent. Hearing in snakes is limited to the vibrations transmitted from the ground via the jaw bones to the skull, and to airborne sounds of low frequency. The eyes differ as well. Most Saurians have movable eyelids, which enables them to

▲ Slough of a grass snake

close their eyes, while the Serpentes have permanently open eyes which are protected from outward danger by a transparent membrane called the 'spectacle' or brille. The eyes of snakes and lizards further differ in structure and focussing ability.

The Squamata have the following features to differentiate them from other reptiles: reduced skull, particularly in the temporal region; transverse and not longitudinal anal aperture, as in the case of the tortoises and turtles, and crocodiles; paired copulatory organs; presence of a series of sensitive buccal cells (Jacobson's organs); egg tooth present in young; glands present in two species of lizard and in numerous snakes. The Sauria have an extremely wide

Chameleon
Chamaeleo dilepis ▶

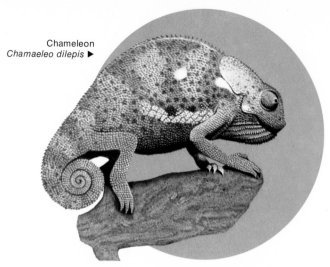

▼ Giant Galapagos tortoise *Geochelone elephantopu*
and a small Madagascan tortoise *Geochelone radia*

▲ A komodo dragon *Varanus komodoensis*

variety of forms, unlike the Serpentes, ranging from the lacertid lizards which are abundant in Europe and move nimbly and briskly, to the spiny *Moloch horridus* or thorny devil found in the hot and arid deserts of Australia, and from the chameleons with their opposable digits, independently rotating eyes and prehensile tails to the burrowing limbless skinks.

As a class, reptiles come in a variety of shapes and sizes. Where tortoises and turtles are concerned, the extremes are represented by the mud-dwelling musk terrapin which may reach 10 cm in length (*Kinosternon subrubrum*), and the leathery Turtle which reaches over 2 metres and lives on jellyfish. It normally inhabits tropical seas but occasionally becomes stranded on the shores of Western Europe. There is also the giant Galapagos tortoise (the largest of all terrestrial Testudines) which measures about a metre in length and can weigh up to 200 kg.

The giant among the crocodiles of almost 7 metres is the Orinoco crocodile (*Crocodylus intermedius*). Reports of larger sized crocodilians are now believed to be ill-founded and even the Saltwater crocodile (*C. porosus*) which was once thought to be the largest species probably attains no more than 6 metres. As far as the Saurians are concerned, the range in size is truly vast: from certain Gekkonidae measuring just 5 cm to the enormous giant komodo dragon

▲ Green mamba *Dendroaspis angusticeps*

or karbara goya (*Varanus komodoensis*) measuring 3 metres, which can even kill small mammals as food.

Among the Ophidia the largest-sized species are those belonging to the families Boidae and Elapidae. Anacondas measure up to 11 metres, pythons up to 10 metres and boa constrictors up to 5.5 metres. Also, the extremely poisonous Hamadryad or king cobra measures up to 5.5 metres. The smallest species are almost all members of the Leptotyphlopidae (with specimens no longer than 38 cm when adult).

When discussing dimensions, it should be remembered that for reptiles, as well as for certain amphibians, growth is not brought to a halt by the attainment of sexual maturity, but carries on, albeit at a slower rate, until each individual eventually dies.

The skin and its features
Of the various and differently developed adaptations that enabled the reptiles to live on this planet up to the Mesozoic Era, the most essential and important were undoubtedly the amniotic egg and the skin. The function of the skin is primarily to conserve water and to protect the animal from

▲ Boa constrictor *Constrictor constrictor*

injuries caused by the reptile's environment. In some cases the skin also serves as a defence against enemies of the snake by possessing coloration and pattern that help conceal the snake from its predators. Special structures, such as thorn-like spines on the nose and eyelids in some species,

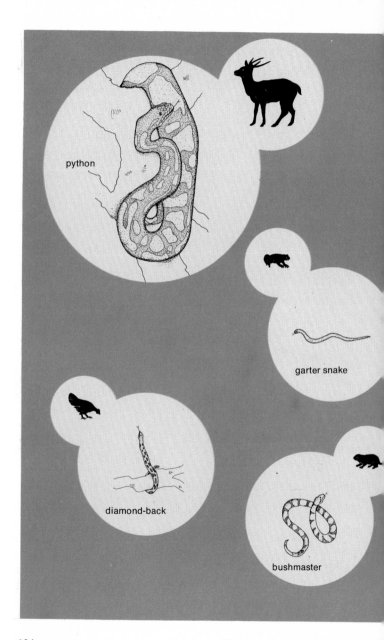

The prey of some typical snakes ▲

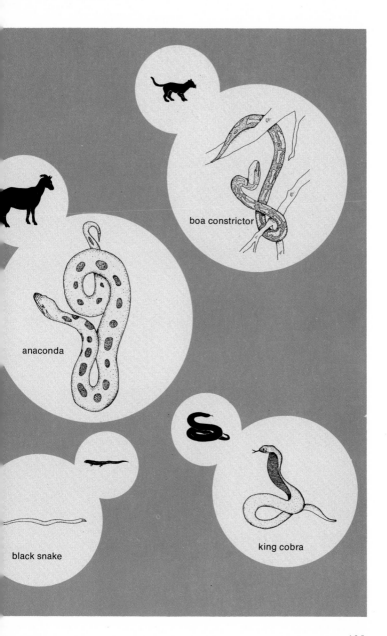

boa constrictor

anaconda

black snake

king cobra

further disguise them. An additional function of the skin is to facilitate the snake's progress on land. Most terrestrial snakes have a row of broad scales along their undersurface, each scale corresponding with a vertebra, and by the thrusts exerted by muscles attached to the belly skin and the ribs the snakes creep along the ground.

The skin of reptiles is essentially dry, scaly and almost completely gland-less. It is formed by two basic layers: the

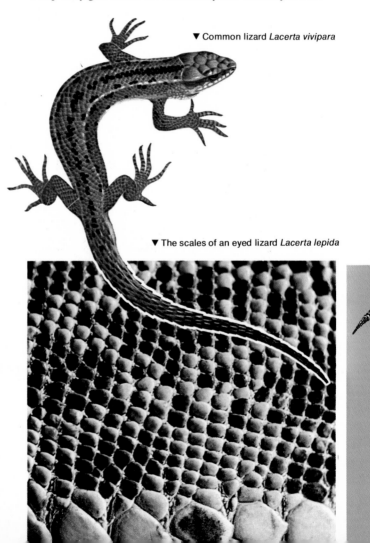

▼ Common lizard *Lacerta vivipara*

▼ The scales of an eyed lizard *Lacerta lepida*

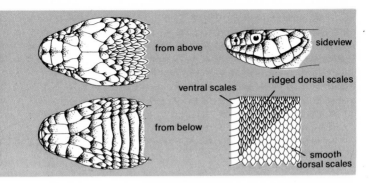

from above

sideview

ridged dorsal scales

ventral scales

from below

smooth dorsal scales

▲ The head of a grass snake   ▲ Detail of a snake's trunk

epidermis, which has a horny outer layer, and the dermis which houses the pigment cells, nerves and blood vessels.

The uppermost layer of the epidermis is arranged in the form of scales. Although to all appearances they may look detached, they are actually only a series of thickenings of the integument caused by keratinizing the uppermost layers of the epidermis itself. These layers continue uninterrupted from one scale to another, and tend at most to grow thinner at points corresponding to the area of separation between one scale and the next. It is this aspect which gives almost all

▼ A Nile crocodile viewed from the side and below

these creatures (excluding the tortoises and turtles) a certain flexibility in their movements.

The number, shape and size of the scales may differ from species to species and the scale pattern often provides a useful means of identification. Generally speaking the scales of snakes and of some lizards form large symmetrical plates on the head. These are in marked contrast to the small body scales. The ventral scales are broadly enlarged and slightly overlapping and as has already been mentioned, have a locomotive function by increasing the animal's grip on the ground. What is more, and this again depends on their

▲ The hinged plastron of a box turtle

position on the animal's head and body, the scales often have pits and tubercles that have tactile and heat sensitive functions. The innermost layer of skin contains the pigment cells (chromatophores) which are responsible for the reptile's colour pattern and ability to change colour. The most common type of cell is known as melanophore as it contains the dark brown pigment melanin.

Some reptilian scales are supported by bony plates (such as in crocodiles and skinks). Beneath the horny plates covering the shell of tortoises and turtles is a bony 'box'

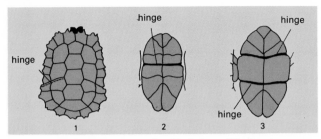

▲ (1) Carapace of the African tortoise; (2) plastron of the American box terrapin; (3) plastron of the freshwater mud terrapin

▲ American box terrapin *Terrapene carolina*

Tarente *Agama stellio* ▶

▼ Plumed basilisk *Basiliscus plumbifrons*

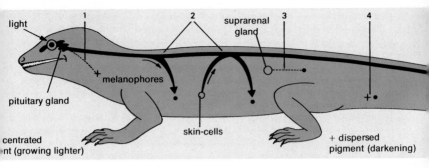

light

1

2

suprarenal
gland

3

4

pituitary gland

melanophores

skin-cells

centrated
nt (growing lighter)

+ dispersed
pigment (darkening)

▲ Methods of melanophore control in a reptile subjected to a light stimulus:
(1) action of pituitary gland on melanophores; (2) nerve control of melanophores via
spinal cord or skin cells; (3) nervous stimulus causes adrenalin to activate
melanophores; (4) melanophores responding directly to light stimulus

which consists, dorsally, of the carapace to which the ribs
and vertebrae are fused. It can be seen to be made up of a
series of plates: one central or vertebral series, flanked on
either side by costal plates and on their outer border by
marginal plates which meet both in front and at the rear.
The ventral shell (plastron) is similarly formed by a series of
plates. There are, of course, numerous variations on this
theme: not only in terms of the number, size and form of the
individual plates, but also in terms of the overall shape and
convexity of the carapace. It is generally flattish in the
aquatic forms to meet the need for greater hydrodynamic or
streamlined efficiency. It tends to be conspicuously rounded
in the terrestrial forms (although the *Malacochersus tornieri*,
or pancake tortoise, an African species adapted to living in
rock crevices, has a thin scutum). In some case the carapace
may be smooth, in others carinate or ridged, and in some
forms with hinges made of connective or cartilaginous tissue
at the lateral borders or front of the plastron. The
development of each single horny plate entails growth in
every direction, starting from a central embryonic section.
The concentric lines usually visible on the plates give an idea
of the age of the animal in question. One of the few species
that do not have horny scutes covering the bony carapace is
the giant leatherback turtle (*Dermochelys coriacea*). In this
species the carapace is not only separate from the skeleton
(which is unique among the members of this Order) but also
formed by a large number of small polygonal plates, or
laminae, fitted together and covered by a leathery layer.

111

The scutum and plastron of the leathery turtle (also called the leatherback and luth) have, respectively, seven and five lengthwise ridges. The shell of the matamata (*Chelys fimbriata*), a South American aquatic species measuring some 20 cm in length resembles a small pile of dry leaves because of its rough appearance and ridges. The snout has a long snorkel-like proboscis, at the end of which lie the nostrils.

Sloughing

All the Squamata periodically slough the thin and transparent horny layer of skin which covers the scales. The frequency of slough varies with the species and the maturity of the individual. Since the necessity to slough is partly to allow for growth young individuals shed their skin more frequently (up to seven times each year) than older animals. The skin of Saurians drops off in irregularly shaped pieces, and the animal helps this operation by tearing off the old skin with its teeth or rubbing its body against a stone or plant. In the case of the snakes, the old skin is sloughed in one piece but turned inside out. Shortly before sloughing begins the animal becomes sluggish, its colours lose their sheen and brightness, and the eyes turn cloudy. It rejects all food, displays irritability, and aquatic forms may spend much of their time in water, probably to help soften the old skin and make it easier to shed.

By rubbing its face and head against stones or other types of rough surfaces the snake breaks the surface layer of its skin around the lips and then starts to peel it off like a garment that has become too tight. Once the jaw area has been negotiated, the slough comes away altogether, peeling back like the finger of a glove.

After sloughing has taken place, snakes and lizards move about nimbly, start eating once more, and look as if they have been freshly 'painted' with bright and sometimes iridescent colours.

The skin formations

Unlike other vertebrates (such as fishes, amphibians and mammals) reptiles – like birds – have a very small number of skin glands. In reptiles these glands are situated in clearly defined areas and are associated with sex discrimination and defence. The musk terrapins have glands under the chin and beneath the margin of their carapace, which secrete a

Skin of a snake during sloughing: (1) at rest; (2–3) before sloughing; (4) sloughing

1

horny layer

zone that loosens

3

2

4

sloughed skin

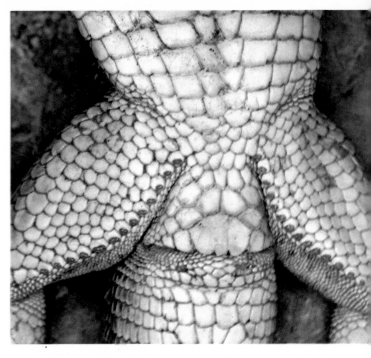

▲ Cloacal region of a male eyed lizard (*Lacerta lepida*) showing femoral and preanal pores

foul-smelling substance that functions in species recognition. Certain crocodilians also have musk glands, while crocodiles have an additional two rows of tiny glands along their backs which secrete an oily but odourless substance of unknown function.

Many snakes have cloacal glands and some have so-called muchal-dorsal glands with an irritant secretion acting on the mucous membranes. This may be associated with their defence mechanisms or sex recognition.

Among the Saurians, and particularly in certain Lacertidae, Agamidae, Teidae, Gekkonidae and Iguanidae, there are the preanal and femoral pores. Situated in front of the cloacal opening and along the under surface of each thigh, these pores are present in both sexes in the Lacertidae, but only in the male species in the others. One hypothesis about the function of these pores is that they are

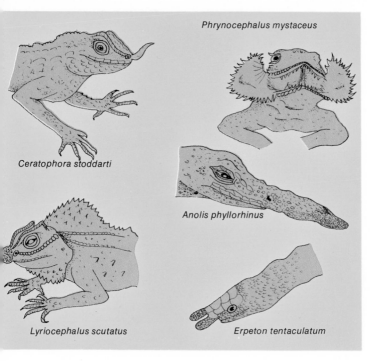

Phrynocephalus mystaceus

Ceratophora stoddarti

Anolis phyllorhinus

Lyriocephalus scutatus

Erpeton tentaculatum

▲ Special skin structures in reptiles

capable, with their secretion, of giving the skin a certain rough, wrinkled quality which prevents there being any possibility of slipping during the mating 'embrace'.

Of the whole class of reptiles, those which have the largest and most varied number of cutaneous appendages are without doubt the Saurians. In fact many chameleons, iguanas and agamids often have distinctive spines, crests, frills and horns. In every instance these are modified scales or skin membranes covered with scales and sometimes supported by skeletal elements. In Europe, for example, the tarente (*Agama stellio*), which is fairly widespread, has a covering formed by two types of scales, some flat, and the others markedly ridged. These latter are gathered in clusters which occur mainly on the legs. Chameleons often have high casques and horns on the head, formed with the help of structures made of bone tissue.

▲ Jackson's chameleon *Chamaeleon jacksoni*

The Australian frilled lizard (*Chlamydosaurus*), flying lizards (*Draco*) and basilisks are noted for the folds and pleats of skin which are invariably brightly coloured and can become remarkably large when used as defence mechanisms.

A similar role can be attributed to the dorsal crests which run along the backs of many members of this group of animals and also appear in the only representatives of the order: Rhynchocephalia, the New Zealand tuataras. Where snakes are concerned only a few Viperidae have small pointed horns on top of their heads, while the Colubrid, *Erpeton tentaculatum* or fishing snake found in South East Asia, has two long and extremely flexible scaly tentacles on its nose. The function of this is somewhat obscure, and the Madagascan *Langaha allaudi* has cephalic extremeties terminating in a conical appendage in the males and a leaf-shaped appendage in the females. The thread-like growths which appear on the head and neck of the matamata, and the worm-like projection from the tongue in the alligator snapping turtles are believed to act as lures. As they sway in water they attract small fishes, tadpoles and crustaceans which are then swiftly swallowed up by the mouth which opens and snaps shut with lightning speed. Some tortoises have horny spurs on their thighs, probably used during mating. The last and most interesting skin

116

▲ Common iguana *Iguana iguana*

formation is the 'rattle' which develops at the tip of the tails of rattle-snakes, found mainly in hot regions in the New world. When the snake vibrates its tail the series of loose horny segments produce a distinctive buzz; this 'rattle' is probably to warn off other animals with whom an encounter, or fight, would result in mutual disadvantage.

Despite the fact that rattle snakes slough their skin as many as three times a year, the length of the rattle is usually

▼ Horned asp *Cerastes cerastes*

limited to about fourteen rings although captive animals may have more. The terminal or oldest rings wear out and drop off naturally.

Lastly, a brief word about the so-called cutaneous armour of reptiles. This feature was present in many primitive and now extinct forms. These formations consist of bony plates which support the horny scales, and are situated within the dermis. Of present-day reptiles, only the crocodilians (crocodiles, alligators, gharial, false gharial), certain Saurians and the tuatara have this type of structure.

The supporting apparatus
The spinal column is formed by a number of vertebrae ranging from 16 in a small Saurian to 500 in a snake. The vertebrae are of the amphicoelous or biconcave type only in the Rhynchocephalia and in many Gekkonidae. In fact this is a primitive feature which does not appear in the other members of the class. The principal type of vertebrae is the procoelous type which is concave in front, and by giving a fairly flexible joint is well suited to the rolling or swaying movement which hallmarks most of the members of this class.

The reptile skeleton is divided into various regions: a set of cervical vertebrae the first of which is connected to the skull by a single condyle; a series of trunk vertebrae with a sacral zone to which the pelvic girdle is attached, and lastly a caudal zone which varies with tail length. With the exception of the giant leatherback turtle, the ribs of the trunk vertebrae in tortoises and turtles are expanded and are joined to the upper shell. As a result of this the central section of the spinal column is completely rigid, and

▼ Skeleton of a tuatara   Skeleton of a snake ▶

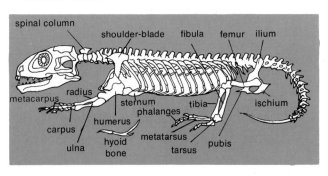

118

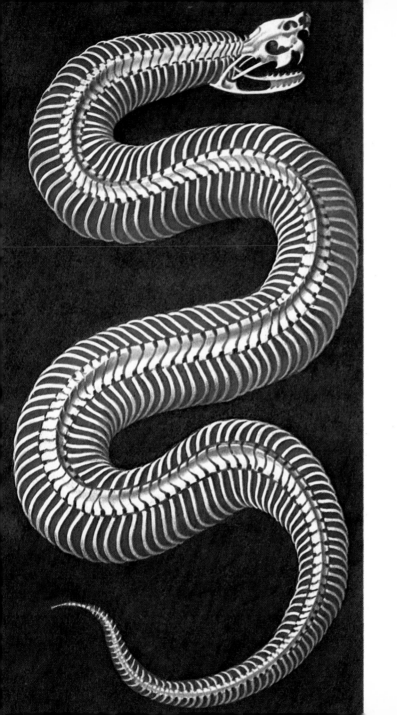

consequently tortoises and turtles do not have the typically swaying or rolling gait of reptiles. This structure also affects the breathing.

In snakes the skeleton has various adaptations associated with the specific way of life (principally movement and feeding) which these creatures lead. With the exception of the first two vertebrae (the atlas and axis) and the caudal vertebrae, the extremely numerous vertebrae all bear ribs. There is no shoulder girdle, and no sternum. The pelvic girdle only features in certain primitive families (Boidae, Typhlopidae, Leptotyphlopidae, Aniliidae).

▼ Skeleton of a flying dragon *Draco volans*

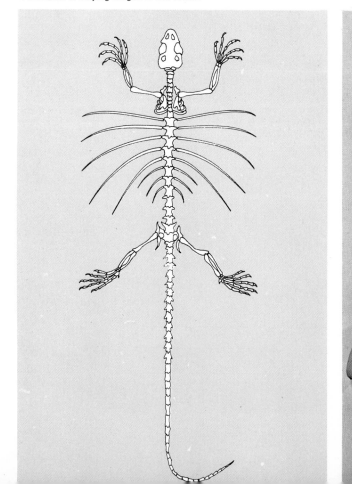

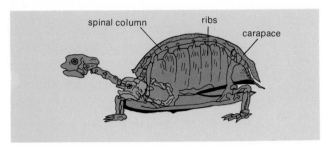

▲ Structure of a tortoise

▼ Skeleton of *Edaphosaurus* (Permian)

In the case of the lizards there is generally a much smaller number of vertebrae and even in leg-less forms the pelvis and shoulder girdle are always present.

The skull varies from Order to Order in shape, dentition and tooth implantation, degree of flexibility, bony components and other features such as the openings referred to below. Except in one genus of snake the skull is joined to the first vertebrae in the spine by means of a single condyle.

Turtles have an anapsid skull with no temporal fossae. Crocodiles and the tuatara have a diapsid skull with two temporal fossae, while the Saurians are modified diapsids. In snakes further modification to the diapsid condition has taken place with loss of the boundaries to the fossae. A basic feature of reptiles is the presence of a quadrate, the bone with which the lower jaw articulates. A movable quadrate is of particular importance to snakes as it increases the gape and assists in the snakes engulfing large prey. Instead of teeth the jaws of adult tortoises and turtles have a horny casing that forms a cutting edge. In the crocodiles, there are teeth on the crests of both upper and lower jaws which are cone-shaped, and set in deep sockets and subject to periodic replacement. In snakes, the teeth differ from family to family, but are generally small, pointed and curved backwards in order to keep a better hold on their prey. The teeth are not situated in separate sockets, but fused to the outer wall of the jaw bone and are subject to frequent replacement. Many species of snakes also have the so-called 'poison fangs', which are dealt with in another section. In Saurians, too, the teeth are small and often numerous, and not situated in separate sockets. In this group of animals, however, and depending on the family, the teeth are either fused to the crests of the jaw bones or, like snakes, to the outer walls of the jaw bones. In those lizards having the latter type of dentition replacement of the teeth is rare. The tuatara has a number of primitive features. The teeth are mostly chisel shaped and fused to the cutting edge on the crests of the jaws. They are non-renewable. The bone at the front of the upper jaw bears one large tooth which is considerably larger than those further back.

The legs in reptiles have the typical structure of all terrestrial vertebrates but with secondary modification for species which have returned to the water or are adapted to a burrowing existence. A shoulder girdle and a pelvic girdle connect the legs to the spinal column. In the tortoises, the legs have five toes and are equipped with strong claws.

SUBCLASS	SKULL	
Anapsida	anapsid	
Lepidosauria	diapsid	
Archosauria		
Parapsida	parapsid	
Ichthyopterygia	metapsid	
Synapsida	synapsid	

Where the turtles are concerned, they have assumed the shape of paddles or flippers which are more suitable for swimming. In the crocodiles there are always four legs, the front having five toes and the hind four. There is a web between all the toes which enables these animals to move swiftly in the water as well. The main function of the massive crocodilian legs is to support the body while the animal moves across dry land.

Snakes and certain Saurians have no legs at all. In most cases, however, the legs of Saurians are well developed and equipped with claws, which help them to get a better grip on the ground. The toes are usually fairly slender and the fourth toe is longer than the others. The arboreal species, such as the chameleons, have pincer-like toes which help them when climbing. Three of the toes oppose the other two, so as to give them a better grip on branches. Supported by the end of the spinal column, the tail comes in different shapes and sizes in the various members of the class. In tortoises and turtles the tail is short and in some cases can be withdrawn inside the shell. There are at least 40 vertebrae in a crocodile's tail; it is laterally compressed and has powerful muscles. Where the Squamata are concerned, some Saurians also have long muscular tails (some 100 vertebrae in the giant komodo dragon) while many snakes, especially primitive species and vipers, have short tails. Even in snakes that have long slender tails, however, the length of the tail is generally less than one third of the overall body length.

The musculature
In all reptiles the muscular apparatus is extremely well developed, both in the aquatic and terrestrial forms.

In the snakes the lateral muscles of the trunk are

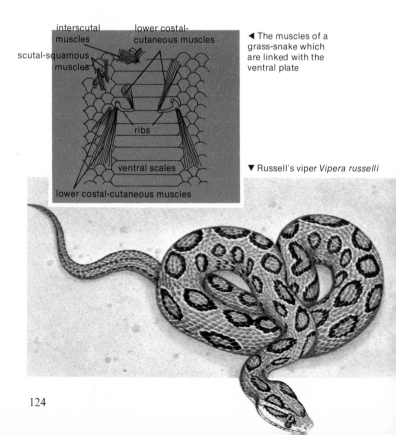

interscutal muscles
lower costal-cutaneous muscles
scutal-squamous muscles
ribs
ventral scales
lower costal-cutaneous muscles

◀ The muscles of a grass-snake which are linked with the ventral plate

▼ Russell's viper *Vipera russelli*

responsible for the undulatory movements of the body. The slow movements are made with the help of muscles that connect with the ventral scales; each one of these is connected to a pair of very mobile ribs which have a special type of musculature. The alternate mechanisms of contraction and subsequent relaxation give rise to a series of waves which enable the creature to move forward.

Voluntary amputation

In the tuatara, many lizards and amphisbaenians the tail has a special feature. This is that it can be amputated if the animal is attacked by an enemy in that area of its body. All it takes is a fairly mild jerk to make most of the tail part company with the rest of the body. When this occurs the muscles in the tail-stump contract and cause in it a series of vibrations which attract the attention of the predator and divert his eye from the real prey, which by then is tail-less. Most of the forms that can shed their tails are able to produce a new tail within a relatively short time and these 'second' tails are easily identifiable as they are a different pattern and colour. Sometimes, if the original tail is not completely lost but only torn loose in one spot, a new tail may still emerge just the same from the wound. It is possible that a lizard may have two tails. The breaking-off of the tail takes place along a predetermined fracture plane which

▼ Superficial musculature of a tuatara

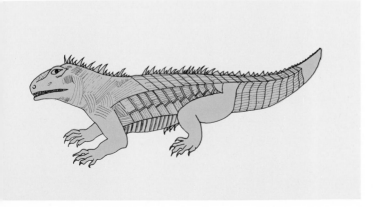

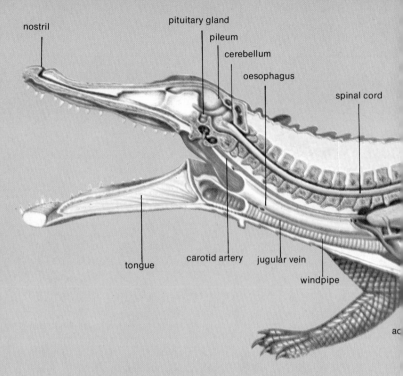

nostril

pituitary gland

pileum

cerebellum

oesophagus

spinal cord

tongue

carotid artery

jugular vein

windpipe

ac

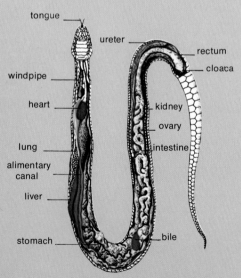

tongue

ureter

rectum

cloaca

windpipe

heart

kidney

ovary

lung

intestine

alimentary
canal

liver

stomach

bile

▲ Anatomy of female grass snake, genus *Natrix*

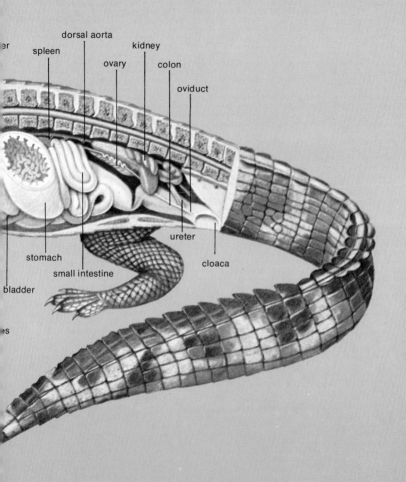

spleen

dorsal aorta

ovary

kidney

colon

oviduct

ureter

cloaca

stomach

small intestine

bladder

▲ Anatomy of female alligator, genus *Alligator*

passes through the middle of the vertebrae, and not in between two vertebrae. Those species that can shed their tails have a series of fracture planes in most tail vertebrae except those towards the tail base.

The Gekkonidae are particularly adept at throwing off their tails at a fracture plane. Some other lizards and a few amphisbaenians, however, merely have fragile tails that may break off *between* vertebrae and when this happens it is not usual for tail regeneration to occur.

The internal organs

The reptiles which, more than any other, present a well developed internal organization and structure are the crocodiles. These are amniotic animals, because of the presence of the amnion which envelops the embryo. They are also poikilothermic vertebrates, tetrapods (four-footed) and scaled. The digestive apparatus, together with the accompanying large glands (liver and gall-bladder), is adapted to an occasionally herbivorous, and sometimes carnivorous diet, the latter being more usual. The breathing apparatus consists of lungs capable of absorbing atmospheric oxygen, in accordance with their essentially terrestrial environment. The circulatory system is also far more complex than in amphibians. The size of the septum, which separates the two ventricles in the heart, gradually increases from the less evolved forms of reptiles, such as tortoises and turtles, to the more evolved forms, such as the crocodiles. As far as crocodiles are concerned, venous and arterial blood are no longer inter-mixed.

The maintenance of a certain water-balance is essential to the survival of these animals, and it is possible to attribute three major rôles to this feature. Firstly, in the blood, the lymph and the interstitial fluids of the tissues, there is a fairly low concentration of mineral salts, which will guarantee that the cells do not die. Secondly, body-temperature is regulated by dispersing or collecting heat by means of evaporation mechanisms. Thirdly, the elimination of waste caused by metabolic activities, by means of the kidneys.

Adaptations for the return to water

The fact that they managed to make their way on to dry land and free themselves from their original aquatic habitat was undoubtedly a very important victory for the reptiles. In fact the reasons that summoned them on to dry land (the possibility of a better chance of survival because of there being more food, a more favourable climate, and fewer competitors) later caused some members of the class to return to the water, both salt and freshwater. Obviously the physical, chemical and climatic differences offered by these two types of environment have given rise to numerous modifications in the morphology and structures of those animals who made the return visit.

The most important modification is their size. Because water is much denser than air, animals living in water are in no way at a disadvantage if their size increases. Think, for example, of the bulkiness of certain species of sea-turtles and certain members of the crocodile group. Size is associated with the problem of movement which, in a denser medium, is obviously more difficult. Another function which is considerably affected by the aquatic environment is breathing, because the lungs of terrestrial creatures are not capable of absorbing the oxygen released in water. Lacking the gills with which fishes or the aquatic larvae of amphibians are equipped, certain reptiles use their skin or the mucous membranes which line the pharynx and cloaca to breathe in water.

Another different adaptation required by the two environments concerns the renal or kidney function, which is the excretion of waste produced by metabolic activity. In water the elimination of these substances is much simpler because the problem of saving the precious fluid does not apply. Excreta are therefore released directly into the water, as happens with mammals, whereas in the case of the terrestrial forms of this class, the water is always reabsorbed by the creature so that it can be re-used.

Because their eggs might run the risk of sinking gradually to the bottom as they are laid, the aquatic reptiles either return to *terra firma* to lay their eggs (as turtles do) or give birth to live young which can already swim (as most sea-snakes do).

Only two kinds of snake are known to eat crabs, both of them being mildly toxic freshwater homalopsines: *Fordonia*, which lives in S.E. Asia, and the Australasian *Myron*. Crustaceans also figure in the diet of non-venomous species, such as the American natricine snakes genus *Regina* and the Asiatic *Psammodynastes* who are both crayfish eaters. The reptiles best adapted to an aquatic environment (both fresh and salt-water) are the terrapins, sea turtles, crocodilians and some groups of snakes, notably the S.E. Asian Acrochordidae, certain Colubridae, the sea-snakes in the family Elapidae and certain Crotalidae. Among the Saurians the only marine creature is the Galapagos sea iguana (*Amblyrhynchus cristatus*) which only takes to the sea in order to feed on certain types of seaweed.

129

How Reptiles Live

Body metabolism

One of the most remarkable features of the reptiles is the slow rate of their metabolism when compared with, for instance, that of a mammal of the same weight. This extraordinarily slow rate affects their whole existence as well as the correct development of all their vital functions.

Thus, even though recent research has shown that the energy used by a lizard while running is comparable to that used by a mouse or squirrel moving at the same speed, the time that the lizard must devote to resting, which is essential if it is to recover the energy spent while running, is far greater than that needed by the mouse or squirrel to the same end.

Because reptiles have a lower metabolism than that of so-called 'warm-blooded' animals, their energy requirements are less and therefore they do not have to spend so much time or energy hunting for food.

Perhaps the most inert and sluggish members of the entire class are the snakes. These creatures spend most of their time

half-asleep, and the only stimuli that can rouse them from their state of torpor are hunger-pangs (due to a prior period of fasting, due in turn to laziness) and sex. Wrapped around a branch or hidden beneath a stone, they will remain motionless for days on end, and sometimes even for weeks on end, without bothering to eat, just managing to breathe, and at most flicking out their highly sensitive tongue to glean, from the surrounding environment, any possibly useful information which might affect their survival.

Feeding
One of the attractive features of dry land, which was also one of the reasons for the success of these animals from the remote Mesozoic Era onwards, was the plentiful abundance of insects available there in comparison with the earth's waters which were filled by many rivalry-ridden species.

In fact before they learnt to feed on amphibians and their smaller kin, the large prehistoric reptiles were insectivores.

This food habit has been retained right up to the present day by their descendants which, independently of their future preferences, feed exclusively on insects when newly born. However, as adults the diets of this class embrace a vast range of possibilities: fruit, leaves and young shoots and buds for the vegetarian arboreal species; insects for those which remain insectivores as adults as well (sometimes with marked preferences for certain species such as ants or termites); various aquatic creatures for the aquatic species; and warm-blooded prey (such as birds and mammals) for the more typical carnivores. In addition the snakes which feed solely on eggs are of particular interest.

The organization and structure of the digestive apparatus entail the whole series of organs (oesophagus, stomach, intestine) and glands (buccal glands, liver and pancreas, to name just the most important of them) which exist in vertebrates. The elements which tend to differ from species to species in the various Orders, and sometimes even within the same Order from species to species, are the formation of the mouth, the tongue and the teeth. These three formations are closely linked with the type of food and, therefore, with the typical habitat of the various animals.

As previously explained tortoises, terrapins and turtles have no teeth but instead have a horny beak which covers the jaws, and which has sharp cutting edges like the blade of a knife. This beak does not shred the food, but simply cuts it into fairly large pieces. The terrestrial species are generally vegetarian, or at most fond of small invertebrates (insects, slugs, snails and worms). The freshwater species are carnivorous as a rule, but some also eat aquatic plants. Most of the marine species feed on jellyfish and small crustaceans but the green turtle is primarily a seagrass feeder.

Unlike the other members of the class which, if carnivorous, feed only and exclusively on live prey, the freshwater turtles (terrapins) may occasionally take dead prey, and thus make an important contribution to the maintenance of the biological equilibrium of the environment in which they live. Another special feature is the layer covering the oesophagus which is formed by strange horny papillae.

The exception of the rule, where this group is concerned, is represented by the members of the family Trionychoidea, or soft-shelled mud tortoises. Probably as the result of the absence of horny plates in the carapace, these creatures also have no beak. Instead they have two fairly pronounced and

▼ Inset: the 'beak' of the freshwater terrapin *Batagur baska*

fleshy lips. The mud tortoises are extremely agile hunters, and have been known to attack fairly large vertebrates such as fishes, amphibians, reptiles and even birds.

Tortoises and turtles generally catch their prey with the help of the special musculature with which their strong jaws are equipped. However, the matamata sports decoy-like appendages on its head which act as lures for the small fishes on which it feeds. Similarly, the alligator terrapin or turtle, which lives in rivers in the south-eastern United States has its own distinctive decoy on its tongue. With the mouth wide open the pink lure attracts fish and as they swim into the mouth the jaws snap shut and trap the prey.

Biting is the commonest technique for catching prey among the tortoises and turtles, but the matamata shows a different system for catching food which quite closely resembles that used by fishes. Because its jaw-bones are so weak, it is unable to seize hold of its potential victims. Assisted by its very long neck, the matamata thrusts its head

▼ The matamata *Chelys fimbriata*

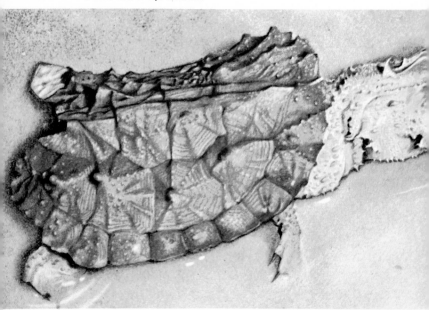

forward whenever anything edible draws close, and dilates its mouth a great deal. The suction thus caused carries the edible morsels, along with a surge of water, into the mouth. A consequence of this fact is that, in this species, the prey are swallowed whole.

The ability of snakes to open the jaws to 180° enables them to swallow large prey which is engulfed head-first. The joints of the upper jaw bones are extremely loose. These work together with a complex system of muscles and ligaments to give a mobility that permits the ingestion of fairly large animals. A large python, measuring some four metres in length would have no difficulty devouring a small pig weighing 27 kilos! However, to facilitate the ability of these animals to greatly dilate their mouths, the quadrate bones which, somewhat loosely, link the skull with the mandibles, are pushed outwards. At the same time the two halves of the maxilla, which are joined by an elastic ligament, work independently of each other and alternately

▼ Eastern Diamond rattle snake (*Crotalus adamanteus*) devouring a mouse

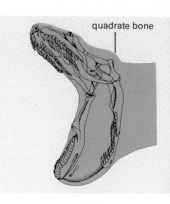

quadrate bone

quadrate bone

▲ The head of a snake with its
jaws tightly closed, and wide open

▼ An egg-eating snake

grip the food and draw it back into the mouth. The sharp, backward curving teeth ensure a tight grip on the victim, as well as a backward progression of the meal.

At the moment of swallowing (deglutition) another mechanism comes into play which prevents any interruption of the breathing; the opening to the windpipe (glottis) is thrust forwards over the tongue and projected from the mouth while its mouth is full.

The last of the adaptations introduced by the carnivorous snakes is that which concerns the techniques for 'tranquillizing' the prey before ingesting it: the venomous species use the venom with which they are equipped for this purpose, by injecting a sufficient dose to immobilise the victim. Many of the non-venomous snakes, on the other

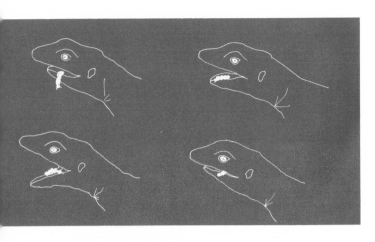

▲ Diagram showing movement of head and jaws of a lizard during inertial feeding

hand, choke their prey by wrapping the coils of their bodies around it. While on the subject of snakes, it is worth mentioning the degree of specialization achieved by the African Dasypeltinae or egg-eating snakes. These snakes swallow and ingest whole eggs; they have cervical vertebrae with cutting edges that penetrate the oesophagus. The projections combined with muscular action puncture the egg as it passes while the yolk and albumen pass directly into the stomach, the pieces of shell are regurgitated.

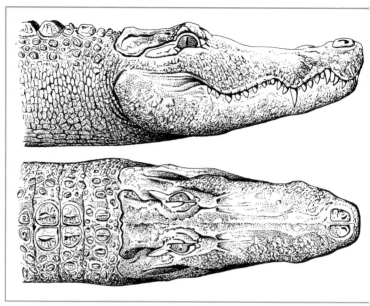

▲ The head of a Mississippi alligator, viewed from the side and from above

Mississippi alligator *Alligator mississipiensis* ▲

The Saurians have adopted a more insectivorous diet than the snakes, but both generally swallow their prey whole, using a mechanism which has been defined 'deglutition by inertia'. Taking hold of the victim, the jaws make a series of movements which 'advance' on the actual prey. In some Saurians, the tail can store reserves of nutritive substances which will then be used in periods when there is a serious food-shortage. It is believed that whole populations of lizards, living on remote islands where the right food is somewhat scarce, have regenerated tails, because of the phenomenon of interspecific cannibalism.

The crocodiles, with their amphibious lifestyle, generally seek out their prey in water. All the members of this Order are carnivores. Once the prey has been caught, it is dragged into the water and held tight by the head or the front legs. The pebbles and stones swallowed by crocodilians act as ballast and their weight in the animal's stomach enables the creature to lie submerged even in fast moving currents, while it overcomes, drowns and devours its prey.

Some of the larger species of crocodiles will also attack human beings. In fact these reptiles are the strongest man-eaters of all the animals on the African continent.

▼ The teeth of an alligator (above) and a crocodile (below)

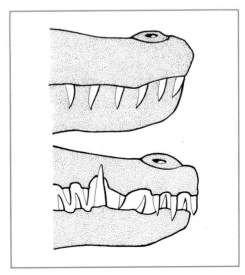

139

The only really harmless species, where man is concerned, is the Indian gavial, or gharial, which eats only fishes.

The tongue

The tongue is a very accurate and vital tool when it comes to catching prey. For some reptiles it not only represents a highly effective hunting weapon but also an excellent instrument of recognition in the face of specific stimuli, mainly chemical in type, offered by the surrounding environment.

This, however, applies essentially to the tongues of two groups of reptiles: the Saurians and the snakes.

In fact in the tortoises and turtles, as in the crocodiles, the tongue is present but never attains that specialized structure and function which it achieves in the other reptilian groups. In tortoises and turtles the tongue is broad, fleshy and directly attached to the floor of the mouth, and is not protrusible. The Saurians, however, have a wide variety of tongues. Sometimes the tongue is fleshy and rounded or blunt at the tip. In a few cases (such as Varamidae and Teidae) it is long, forked and retractile, as in snakes. It is also often brightly coloured, and this feature is sometimes interpreted as an intimidatory device in the face of possible aggressors. In all Saurians the tongue is also covered on the back by papillae and these probably act as taste-buds.

The tongue of the slow-worm is very distinctive. It is believed that it is divided into two sections with different diameters which can be inserted into one another and then evaginated more or less completely, as required.

▼ The floor of the mouth and pharynx of a green turtle

▼ The tongue of a tokay

▼ The tong monitor liz

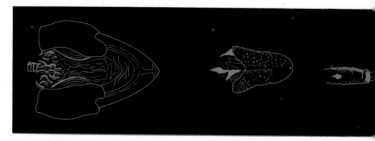

African Rock Python
ython Sebae

▼ The tongue of a slow-worm

▼ The tongue of the Borneo
'earless lizard' *Lanthanotus*

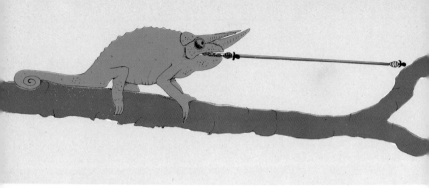

▲ The projection of a chameleon's tongue   A chameleon catching prey ▶

As far as the Saurians are concerned, the chameleon has the most interesting tongue. This animal has a device which can be shot outwards or evaginated to a length equal to one and a half times the overall body-length, excluding the tail. At the front this tongue has a form of club covered with a sticky substance with which the chameleon manages to trap not only insects but also small birds and reptiles. The 'shaft' which supports the tip is a kind of hollow tube which, when at rest, remains folded (like an accordion) on a pointed cartilaginous appendage. This is part of the hyoidal apparatus, which is a series of cartilages and small bones which help to form the supporting framework of the pharynx. As they approach their prey, chameleons hold their heads forward; then suddenly, at lightning speed, they shoot out their tongue towards the victim with amazing accuracy. They then pull in their tongue together with the prey stuck to the end.

Two groups of muscles are essentially responsible for this entire mechanism. Firstly muscles which run along the tongue and which adjust the gathered resting position and the position of recovery; and secondly a set of circular muscles within the walls of the tongue itself which are responsible for the projection of the tongue, by means of the contraction. Unlike most lizards, where the tongue is only projected when catching prey, the tongue of snakes has a rôle not so much as a hunting tool but more as an instrument for recording relevant information from the environment. In shape it is invariably slender and forked. In addition a small groove at the tip of the upper jaw allows the snake to

▲ A spectacled caiman *Caiman crocodylus*

flick its tongue in and out even when the mouth is shut.
When at rest, the tongue is withdrawn into a sheath at the
back of the mouth.

The mucous and sticky secretions which envelop the
tongues of all reptiles are produced by buccal glands which
are generally positioned on the outer edges of the jaws in
Saurians and snakes; in front of the lower jaw and in the
corners of the mouth in tortoises and turtles; and on the
palate and beneath the tongue in crocodiles.

Breathing
The main respiratory organs in reptiles are, typically, the
lungs which form during the development of the embryo and
start to function from the creature's earliest days. Naturally
enough the various environmental demands bring other
respiratory structures into play in this essential function.

inner nostril
(choana)

▲ The soft-shelled turtle *Trionyx formosus*
Inset: roof of the mouth of a green turtle

Before it reaches the pulmonary sacs, however, the inhaled air must negotiate a series of obligatory passages which, in essence, are identical to those which characterize the breathing apparatus in mammals. These consist of the nose (which opens outwards in the form of two nostrils), the pharynx, the larynx, the trachea or windpipe, the bronchial tubes and lastly the lungs. Generally situated at the tip of the snout, the nostrils vary their position in many members of this class. In the 'amphibious' reptiles, such as the crocodiles and water-snakes, the nostrils are placed very high up on the head to enable these animals to breathe atmospheric oxygen even when they are underwater, while in certain strictly aquatic turtles, such as the Trionychoidea (mud tortoises) and the matamata, these nasal apertures are set on top of a long proboscis. This enables them to breathe with just a tiny part of their body showing above the surface of the water.

In this respect it is also as well to mention that almost all the aquatic reptiles have systems designed to shut off the back apertures of the nostrils, and these systems come into use when the animal is submerged.

In the case of the crocodiles the air entering the nostrils is channelled into two long ducts, separated from the mouth by a secondary bony palate. Both in front and behind, these nasal ducts have 'shut-off' valves, which can be set in motion by muscles to prevent the inflow of water into the respiratory system.

In tortoises and turtles there is a different mechanism, which is regulated by the highly vascularized connective tissue which covers the vestibule of the nose. Closure of the nostrils is thus due to the filling, and the consequent swelling, of the connective blood-lacunae. It is probable that the water-snakes and certain desert-dwelling Saurians also use the same system, the former to prevent the entry of water and the latter the entry of sand into the breathing apparatus. Among the Saurians, the komodo dragon and other monitor lizards also have a personal method of regulating their oxygen intake. In these cases the nasal vestibule is very elongated and due to the mucus which lines the numerous cavities in its bony walls, is particularly adapted to retaining tiny particles of air, thus creating something tantamount to a kind of reserve for times when it is most needed (for example during the act of swallowing). The pharynx also varies considerably in its structure in the class as a whole, and as a rule it is rounded off by either muscular laminae, or alternatively by a series of cartilaginous or cutaneous membranes.

The glottis is of crucial importance, inasmuch as it is the natural means of access to the actual respiratory organs; it is like a window which can be opened to varying degrees by means of the actions of special groups of muscles (it is systematically closed in tortoises and turtles and in water-snakes when their head is under the water).

The larynx, which does not differ very much from member to member in this class, leads into the trachea or windpipe which, with the exception of the snakes, forks in relation to the large bronchial tubes which support the lungs.

From the structural viewpoint, it should be noted that the windpipe itself is invariably reinforced by cartilaginous rings, except in the case of snakes. Because of the fact that their long bodies rest directly on the ground, they have replaced the cartilaginous rings on the belly with a band of more elastic connective tissue.

The lungs are formed by a series of increasingly complex concamerations. The tuatara and the Saurians have the simplest of all lung-structures. It consists of a sac with a single central cavity connected to the bronchial tube, and the alveoli which are directly linked with the aperture in this large sac. The chameleons, however, have a kind of pulmonary sac which resembles the air-sacs of birds. These enable them to puff themselves up with air in order to intimidate any possible attacker.

In all advanced snakes there is only one functional lung, which is the right one. The left lung is either absent or very poorly developed. It has been suggested that the reduction is due to the lack of space caused by the elongation and narrowness of the body of these animals. There are nevertheless primitive species which have two functional lungs, though the left one tends to be less developed than the right. This applies to most members of the Boidae.

Tortoises, turtles and crocodiles have pulmonary structures fairly similar to those of mammals.

In Saurians and snakes the respiratory mechanism entails movements of the ribs and the intercostal musculature. To some extent the absence of a diaphragm limits these respiratory movements. Turtles and terrapins have a very distinctive type of respiration. They introduce water through the cloaca and use the oxygen released from it by absorbing it by means of two highly vascularized inner lateral sacs.

Closely allied with the respiratory mechanism is the peculiar capacity which certain reptiles have of hissing in moments of considerable tension. To do this, air is brusquely expelled from the glottis. In some species we also find an epiglottis which amplifies the sound of the outflow of air by rising and falling. In addition to hissing, some snakes expel air from the cloaca and in so doing make a popping noise; others stridulate by rubbing their coiled bodies against their rough scales. Other reptiles which can produce sounds are the Crocodylia, and in particular the American alligator and certain Gekkonidae among the Saurians.

Circulation and excretion
Like their amphibian ancestors which came before them on the evolutionary ladder, the reptiles have a double and incomplete circulatory system, due to the fact that their heart is also formed by two atria (the left one which collects the blood flowing back from the lungs which is, as a result, rich in oxygen, and the right atrium which, on the contrary, receives the

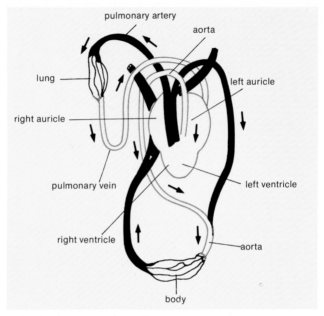

pulmonary artery

aorta

lung

left auricle

right auricle

pulmonary vein

left ventricle

right ventricle

aorta

body

▲ The circulatory system in reptiles

returning blood from the various areas of the body which it has irrigated) and a single ventricle, which is partly divided by a septum.

This situation, however, is peculiar only to the tortoises and turtles, the Saurians and the snakes. In these animals, therefore, the oxygenated blood is, at least to some extent, mixed with the blood which contains little oxygen.

In the crocodiles, on the other hand, we find a separation at the ventricular level. The pulmonary artery, which carries deoxygenated blood to the lungs, leads off the right ventricle, as does the left aorta which then divides and subdivides again and again and distributes blood throughout the body. The right aortic arch leads off the left ventricle. The two branches of the aorta are not yet completely separated from one another, and are linked by the so-called foramen of Panizza. An interesting feature in the reptiles is the mechanism which governs excretion and hence the water-balance in their bodies.

Because, in fact, they cannot permit themselves any water wastage, precisely because of their original attempt to live on dry land, rather than eliminate the waste products produced by the various metabolic activities in acqueous solutions (as the mammals do), these animals reabsorb the water at the cloaca, and eliminate a pasty kind of urine which contains a large amount of uric acid. From the structural viewpoint, the excretory apparatus consists of two elongated kidneys, situated symmetrically at the sides of the spinal column, in which the structure and organization are considerably more complex than in the amphibians. They may be smooth, as in the case of most Saurians, or lobate, as in the tortoises and turtles, the snakes and the alligators. Unlike the other members of the class, the snakes have their kidneys situated one above the other.

The kidneys are connected to the cloacal cavity by two tubes, called the ureters. In male animals, the cloacal cavity also receives the products produced by the testes. The urinary bladder only occurs in the Testudines (tortoises and turtles), the tuatara, and in most Saurians. It is absent in the geckos, iguanas and monitor lizards, as well as in the snakes and crocodiles. In all these animals the urine is retained by the cloacal cavity.

The aquatic reptiles do not encounter any major problems when it comes to the need to save and store water. Thus they eliminate a liquid, non-pasty urine, consisting of water in which, depending on the creature, there may be dissolved ammonia or uric acid.

For those species which live in salt-water things are not so simple. Sea turtles, sea-snakes, the Galapagos sea iguanas, certain creatures which live in brackish or coastal waters like the estuarine or Saltwater crocodile *Crocodylus porosus*, and the American alligator (*Alligator mississippiensis*) all live in an environment where the saline concentration is higher that that of the body fluids.

The ensuing danger is that of a progressive loss of these fluids by osmosis. To combat this danger, marine reptiles have special salt glands that regulate the amount of salt in their blood. The sea turtles, in particular, try to reduce any concentration of salt which would inevitably tend to increase as a result of their diet (consisting principally of molluscs, sponges, fish, aquatic flora and jellyfish, according to the species) by means of the activity of the salt glands.

Similar difficulties concerning the balance of water and salt also beset those reptile species which live in desert

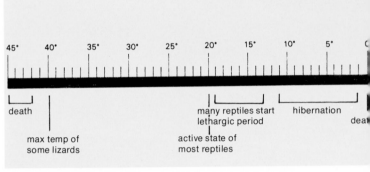

45°   40°   35°   30°   25°   20°   15°   10°   5°   0

death

max temp of
some lizards

many reptiles start
lethargic period

active state of
most reptiles

hibernation

death

▲ Range of temperature necessary to sustain reptilian life

regions, where the availability of water is very slight indeed.
In fact these animals, which cannot dilute the high saline
concentrations in their body fluids with water, also rely on
glandular structures. These consist of nasal glands which can
retain, and later eliminate, excess amounts of potassium
salts.

Body temperature
Like fishes and amphibians, the reptiles are still
heterothermic or poikilothermic animals. In other words,
their bodies cannot maintain a temperature which differs
greatly from the temperature of the environment in which
they live. As a result they can only carry out their various
vital functions when the outside environment supplies them
with a certain degree of heat or warmth. Given the large
number of creatures which belong to this class, and, in
particular, the large number of different habitats in which
they are to be found, the optimum temperature values
suitable for the life and survival of reptiles may vary, from a
minimum of 6°C in the tuatara to a maximum of 40°C.

Within these fairly restricted limits which are, more
importantly, conditioned by the presence of other climatic
factors such as cloudiness, atmospheric humidity, the
thermal conductivity of the bodies in question and so on, the
reptiles, like most living things, alternate periods of activity
with fairly marked and prolonged periods of rest, during
which the metabolism is reduced as far as possible. Logically
enough, the diurnal or daytime reptiles have a better

150

The desert-dwelling
Uromastyx at dawn ▼

▼ The same animal
in the early afternoon

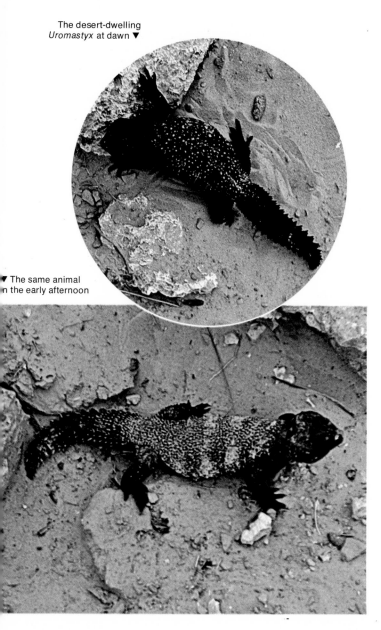

151

▲ Sea iguana *Amblyrhynchus cristatus*

tolerance of higher temperatures than nocturnal species. Lizards and snakes in particular can maintain relatively high and constant body temperatures by making behavioural adjustments, such as moving to and fro between sunny and shady places. They also change their posture to increase or decrease the surface area of their bodies that are exposed. Examples of this include flattening their bodies on warm stones, for instance, or turning up their digits. Several horned 'toads' of the genus *Phrynosoma* make the most of their exceptionally flat bodies by burying themselves in sand in the event of over-exposure to the sun. Working their way backwards, they sink their body beneath the sand and leave just the head exposed. Lacertidae flatten their body to take the most possible heat from the warm rocks on which they rest. In order to cool down the temperature of their bodies,

▲ An asp *Cerastes vipera* burying itself in sand

the terrestrial species take refuge in shady places beneath a plant, or burrow their way into the ground.

In the search for cool environments there is naturally a whole series of different 'anti-heat' techniques. Some reptiles place their bodies parallel with the sun's rays so as to expose the smallest possible body-surface while reducing to the minimum the actual surface itself; others rest their bellies on the ground after having removed the warmer

▼ Dab *Uromastyx acanthinurus*

153

surface earth. A certain Australian lizard Agamidae, stands up on its legs in order to reduce contact with the hot ground.

From the physiological point of view, one of the most frequently employed systems is that of increasing the rate of breathing, and hence the ventilation. Many Saurians change colour in relation to the outside temperature. For instance, *Uromastyx acanthinurus* (the mastigure or dab) is darker in cold conditions and lighter in warm or hot conditions, so that it reflects the hot infra-red rays.

In other instances, where there is no mechanism for changing colour, physiological mechanisms are used which affect the circulatory system. Consequently there is an increase or decrease of the heart-beat according to the need to either warm up or cool down the body-surface.

Movement
Movement in the majority of fossil reptiles was generally clumsy, as a result of a low slung body, short limbs and forward directed digits.

There were once many aquatic species, for example the long-necked Plesiosauria which moved with a slow motion of their paddle-shaped legs and the shark-like Ichthyopterygia with their perfectly streamlined bodies, which could swim by means of thrusts given to the body by the strong tail-fin. The four-footed mammal-like Therapsida had fairly efficient locomotion and were able to move across dry ground with a gait similar to a running motion. The dinosaurs walked on their two hindlegs, while the Pterosauria (pterodactyls) let themselves be swept along by air-currents in long glides, using their wide, wing-like webs that reached from fingers to toes.

Most present-day reptiles have developed longer and more slender limbs. Even though the actual name of the class of 'crawling' animals alludes to a particular type of locomotion, in practice only a small minority of reptiles do crawl. All the various forms of movement depend on the shape and structure of the limbs.

The tortoises have heavy, strong legs which are, therefore, incapable of moving at an agile run and the sea turtles have flippers in place of feet and legs. The crocodiles usually use their tails to move through water and their legs to move on dry land. Among the Saurians there is a huge range of forms, all perfectly adapted to the terrain of the respective environment and often with supplementary structures with cleverly designed specific features.

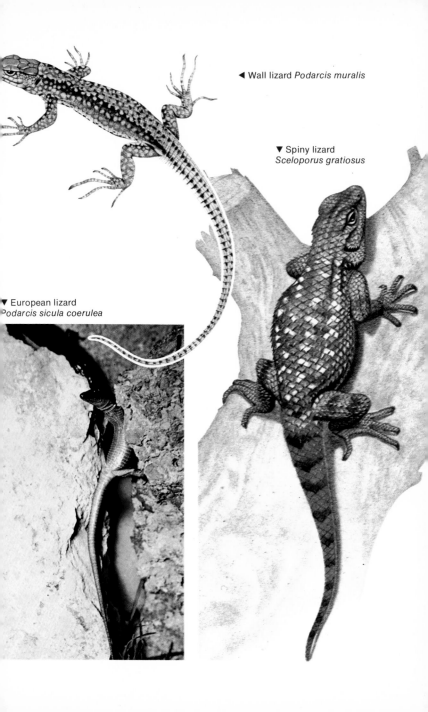

◄ Wall lizard *Podarcis muralis*

▼ Spiny lizard
Sceloporus gratiosus

▼ European lizard
Podarcis sicula coerulea

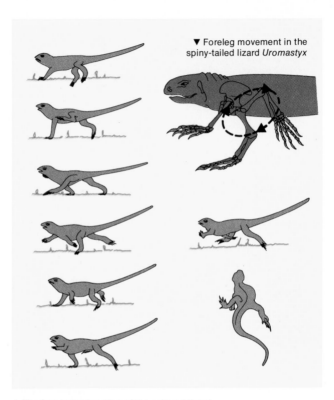

▼ Foreleg movement in the spiny-tailed lizard *Uromastyx*

▲ The four-legged motion of the collared lizard

▼ Nile crocodile *Crocodylus niloticus*

Finally, the leg-less (apodous) snakes move in a variety of ways, almost as if to demonstrate that the presence of legs is not that important a factor in the ability to move.

In order to simplify matters, it is helpful to examine one by one the various types of locomotion used by reptiles, and focus on their most salient features.

Walking and running
The tortoises and turtles, and many short-legged Saurians have a fairly slow gait, in which they move alternately on all four legs. However, when the legs have a longer form, the gait changes from a walk to an actual trot.

Of all the reptiles which have legs, the crocodiles have the greatest number of gaits. They can move slowly forward 'on their stomach' with the legs widely spaced at the side of the body (as their ancestors probably did) or they can advance more quickly with their body raised well above ground-level, and their legs held vertically beneath the actual body, and moved front to back with rhythmic swinging movements. They can even 'gallop', using a synchronized and alternate motion of first the front legs and then the hind legs.

Some Saurians also use a bipedal gait. This applies to many Agamidae, the basilisk lizard, the desert lizard, certain Teiidae (New World lizards) and the Australian monitor lizards. The limbs used in this type of locomotion are the hind legs, counterbalanced by the long tail.

The basilisk lizard is the only creature which manages to continue its two-legged run on water. To facilitate this

▼ A basilisk lizard running

▲ Tokay *Gekko gecko*

The front foot of a gecko ▶
seen from below

movement the toes of its hind-feet are equipped with tiny
lobes. Depending on how smooth the surface of the water
itself is, this run can be maintained for quite some time.
When the basilisk can no longer remain above the surface, it
dives and continues on its way by swimming.

Climbing

Saurians and snakes have, in addition, arboreal habits, which
entail the need to climb, and keep the whole body raised
above the ground.

The chameleons and geckos are pastmasters in the art of
climbing. The chameleons are characterized by having their
toes connected by their skin in such a way that they are
joined in opposable groups, with two toes on one side and
three on the other, thus forming a type of pincer. The tail,
which may be flattened laterally, is long and prehensile in
most species and helps to give the animal a firm hold on
branches. As soon as potential prey has been sighted, and
with what appears to be exasperating slowness, the
chameleon advances one leg at a time, gaining just a few
millimetres and sometimes as little as half a millimetre with
each step. This extremely cautious approach is designed not
to arouse the prey's suspicions.

As far as the Gekkonidae are concerned, many are
excellent climbers and have in addition to claws series of
lamellae under the phalanges. Each one of these is formed
by a vast number of microscopic hooked or branching cells.
By means of special muscles, these cells can be held in a
raised or lowered position, and adhere in this way to
extremely smooth surfaces such as glass. These lamellar
surfaces may be fan-shaped or arranged in lines or rows all
over the surface of the toe. They may also stretch over the
entire breadth of the toe, or have a gap in the central area of
it. In some species, like the leaf-tailed gecko for example,
the tail also has adhesive properties.

In the other families of climbing Saurians, the claws have
the task of ensuring a firm hold and enabling the animal to
move. In most cases they are helped by the tail which is used
as a means of support or as an instrument to grip with.

Another example of an adaptation to climbing along and
up walls is supplied by the Cordylidae. These Saurians are
found mainly in the rocky and craggy regions of South
Africa, and have flattened bodies which enable them to
squeeze their way through the smallest and narrowest cracks
in rocks. They cling to the rocks by means of folds of skin

▲ Boomslang *Dispholidus typus*

equipped with spiny scales which occur on the shoulders, neck and also sometimes on the head.

The last climbing family is the Lacertidae. Despite the fact that members of this family have none of the specialized adaptations of the type hitherto described, they enjoy an arboreal life, and are also found on and in walls and rocks. Their feet often have claws to help grip onto surfaces.

Flying

Closely connected with the arboreal existence we find another feature possessed by certain Saurians and by just one genus of snake, the Oriental *Chrysopelea*. This is the ability to glide.

The lizards best equipped for gliding are S.E. Asian members of the Agamidae, commonly known as 'flying

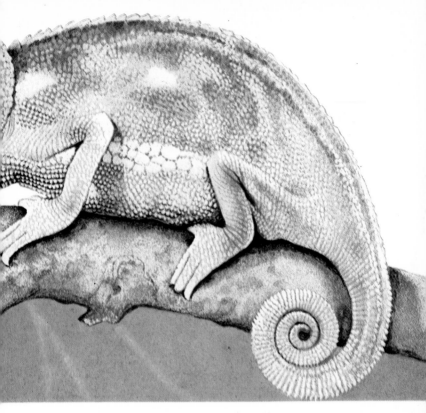

▲ Common chameleon *Chamaeleo chamaeleon*
Inset: left front foot, and section of the tail of an Indian chameleon

dragons' (*Draco*). Between 20 and 40 cm in length, these
slender creatures can glide from branch to branch by
opening, rather like a fan, lateral skin membranes which are
supported by usually five or six pairs of movable ribs which
are greatly elongated and very thin. These 'wings' are folded
against the body when not being used.

Snaking movements
The oddest and most distinctive of all reptilian movements is
'snaking', which enables snakes and some Saurians to move
forward over the ground by means of a series of lateral
undulations of the entire body.

 In general Saurian animals which use snaking movements
have a snake-shaped body, and in the case of the
Amphisbaenia are distinctively 'ringed'. They are often very

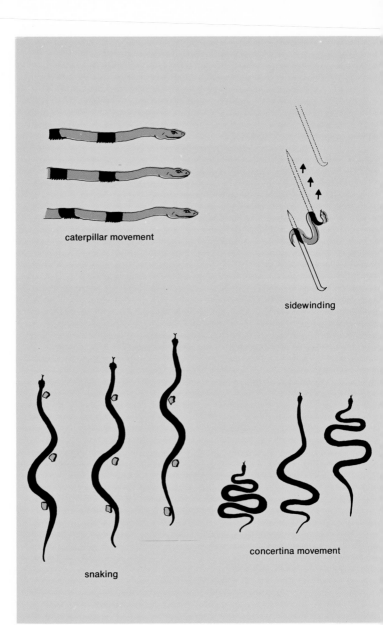

caterpillar movement

sidewinding

snaking

concertina movement

▲ Types of movement in snakes

easily confused with snakes or earth-worms and on the whole lead a subterranean life.

Unlike the other Saurians, certain Amphisbaenia can move their bodies by making not lateral, but vertical undulations.

In the true snakes the snaking movement can be reduced to four basic types:

(1) snaking, during which the body of the animal advances by describing a series of curving movements, with leverage obtained from any tiny irregularity in the surface, such as tufts of grass or stones, protruding roots, or any kind of roughness;

(2) the concertina motion, peculiar to certain smaller species, in which the snake starts from a gathered, resting position, uses its tail as a lever, and thrusts its head and trunk forwards. Finally, using its neck, it pulls the rest of its body along after it;

(3) sidewinding, typical in certain Viperidae (rattle-snakes and vipers). In this type of locomotion, instead of making the classic snaking movements, the creature advances

▼ River Jack *Bitis nasicornis*

through the desert sand in which it lives by moving itself sideways in relation to the position of its body. In other words, the body stays in a double-S position, and alternates the forward movement of just part of the trunk with brief periods of rest during which it finds points of leverage from which to push itself off for the next step: the result is a very swift, oblique gait;

(4) locomotion along a straight line, typical of the large, heavy-bodied snakes. By this method, the snake's grip on the ground is provided by the large flat ventral scales, while the strong longitudinal musculature of the body drags the body forwards.

Many snakes have arboreal habits. Here too they adopt one of the four basic types of locomotion, depending on the distance and kind of terrain to be covered.

In addition some of the arboreal species have a pair of ridges along each ventral scale which gives them a better grip on branches. When a snake has to bridge a gap between two branches, it contracts the muscles throughout the body, which then stiffens like a stick, until it reaches the other branch. It then simply pulls its body after it by slowly unravelling the coils which held it firmly to the first branch.

There is one final point: with the exception of the sidewinding motion adopted by some vipers and rattle-snakes, the other types of locomotion may be variously used depending on the environment in which the movement takes place or even combined together at the same time in the different parts of the body.

Moving in sand

The most typical and widespread desert-dwelling reptiles are Saurians, and especially members of the family Scincidae (the skinks). The spindle-shaped body; pointed, conical head (sometimes with a shovel-shaped snout); cylindrical tail, which in some species is extremely long; and the often highly polished scales, are all adaptations that greatly simplify smooth progress through and over sand. Generally speaking their legs are very small and unable to support the weight of the body, with the result that the body is kept permanently resting on the ground, and is moved forward by thrusts from the small legs during normal locomotion.

In escape manoeuvres, however, the legs are left hanging limply at the sides of the body which is moved forward with a series of snake-like lateral undulations, produced by the strong musculature.

Sand living reptiles: (left) sand skink (*Neoseps reynoldi*) ▶ and (right) a lacertid (*Acanthodactylus scutellatus*)

▲ Leatherback turtle *Dermochelys coriacea*

Desert dwelling members of the family Lacertidae have fringes of scales along their toes which act as 'snow shoes', increasing the surface area and allowing the lizard to negotiate sandy areas. The *Palmatogecko*, a geckonid which lives in the deserts of Namibia, has strange claw-less toes joined together by a flat, thin piece of membrane.

Burrowing and digging movements
It is the Saurians once again which have the highest percentage of burrowing species: the Amphisbaenia, the Anguidae, the Pygopodidae, the Dibamidae, the Annielhidae and, as previously mentioned, the Scincidae. However, even in other families of lizards some species are adapted to burrowing. The fringe-toed lizards or uma's (family Iguanidae) make a swimming motion through sand, using the flatness of their bodies, the sharp edges of their head, and the movable fimbriae round their toes.

With regard to snakes, the burrowing species mostly belong to primitive families, and as a general rule they have a slender, cylindrical body, covered with smooth scales, and usually a short tail. Internally, most have the rudiments of

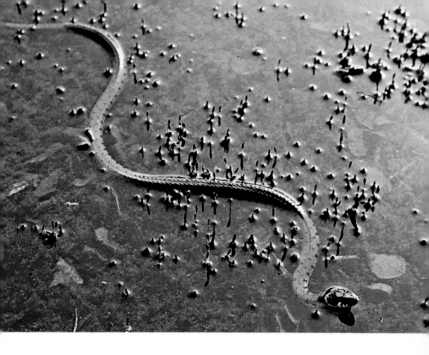

▲ A grass snake *Natrix natrix*

hind legs and a pelvic girdle, and examples showing this are Typhlopidae, Leptolyphlopidae, Aniliidae and Beidae. As a result of the burrowing or digging activity, there is less flexibility of the skull and jaw bones.

Swimming

Contrary to popular belief, the ability to move in water is not common to all the members of this class. The species which lead a wholly aquatic life obviously have body structures which are adapted to swimming, and it is the tail which is the basic and most important element in this type of movement. As the result of its laterally flattened shape, the tail is able to provide propulsion through water. Good examples of this are the crocodiles and, among the aquatic Saurians, certain Varanidae (monitor lizards) and the sea iguanas. The formation of the tail has also been accompanied by certain modifications to the legs, which may be webbed to varying extents. The legs have the job of steering the animal in the desired direction. The aquatic Testudines (turtles and terrapins) are considerably specialized in this respect. Some of the freshwater species

(Emydae and Chelydridae) have webbed toes equipped with well developed claws, and in the soft-shelled Trionychidae the legs are paddle-shaped. In the true sea-turtles, such as the loggerhead turtle and the green turtle which are common in the Mediterranean, the front legs are considerably longer than the hind legs, and have been transformed into flippers which play the leading rôle when these animals swim. The shorter hind legs act as rudders which steer them in the right direction, but in both species these limbs cannot be withdrawn inside the carapace.

Similarly, in the case of the crocodiles, the tail is the main instrument used for swimming and for this reason it is equipped with an especially strong musculature. While the animal swims at high speeds the main function of the legs is to act as stabilizers but otherwise they enable the creature to paddle about in a leisurely fashion.

Among the Saurians the most frequent visitors to water are certain monitor lizards and the sea iguanas. The former prefer rivers in hot regions where they swim with powerful tail-strokes, while sea iguanas are unique among the Saurians since they feed in salt-water. These large reptiles inhabit the Galapagos Islands, and feed exclusively on marine algae which they procure by plunging and diving into the sea with great agility. Again the major swimming instrument here is their large tail. In addition to the animals mentioned already the Saurians include other optionally aquatic forms, such as the basilisk lizards, belonging to the Iguanidae, the caiman lizards (*Dracaena guianensis*) belonging to the Teiidae and the *Hydrosaurus* among the Agamidae.

In the case of the sea snakes, typical salt-water dwellers, the tail is like a large, elongated paddle, while the head and neck are often smaller in diameter than the trunk. This structural feature enables them to make a quick burst of speed when necessary (for example, when about to catch prey). However, the sea snakes very often remain stationary, full-stretch on the surface of the sea, at the total mercy of the waves. The broad abdominal plates which allow the terrestrial species to take a grip on the ground are very much reduced or absent in sea snakes, but like all the freshwater species (such as certain Colubridae, the anaconda among the Boidae, the water mocassins or cottonmouths among the Viperidae), the marine species can remain totally submerged for long periods, taking the oxygen necessary for breathing directly from the water itself.

Co-ordination and information
Taken as a clearly defined systematic class, the class of
reptiles presents a state of cerebral development which is
more advanced than that of members of the less evolved
classes of amphibians and fishes.

As a rule the tortoises and turtles have a fairly small brain,
and it is often considerably smaller than that which could be
contained by the skull. Similarly, the brain of the Loricata is
extremely small when compared with the length of their
bodies. To give some idea of the degree of disproportion
here, a specimen 1 metre in length was found to have a brain
just 5 cm long.

Reptiles' eyes are protected, externally, by two eyelids, a
lower and an upper, which in the snakes and in certain
Saurians, are joined together, transparent, and form the
so-called 'spectacle' which gives them their fixed stare. The
spectacle is periodically replaced when sloughing takes
place. Although it is fixed, it nevertheless gives the eye a
certain amount of mobility. The tortoises and turtles have
small and not very sharp eyes; the crocodiles, conversely,
have very good eyesight. The pupil is vertical as in most
predominantly nocturnal species. There are three eyelids: an
upper, and a lower one, plus a lateral one, this being the
so-called transparent nictitating membrane which stems
from the inner corner of the eye and can close and protect it
if need be (for example, when underwater).

Characterized for the most part by having monocular and
black-and-white vision (experiments appear to have proved
that only certain Agamidae and Lacertidae can distinguish
colours), the eyes of Saurians and snakes have a whole range
of adaptations in relation to their very wide variety of
habitats. In the nocturnal species (as has been already
mentioned in the case of the crocodiles and the tuatara), the
pupil is often elliptical and becomes vertical in the presence
of sudden light, precisely to limit as far as possible the
number of light rays which might bother it if given free rein.

In the Gekkonidae we find cases of vertical pupils with
straight margins (as in cats) or lobate margins, or pupils
equipped with protuberances corresponding to the central
point of each margin. In the light the contraction of the pupil
alters the form: the straight type of margin grows thinner
and finer, assuming the form of the eye of a needle; the
lobate-edged pupil contracts into a series of four vertical
apertures or slits, also resembling the eye of a needle, each
of which produce their image on the retina, at the back of

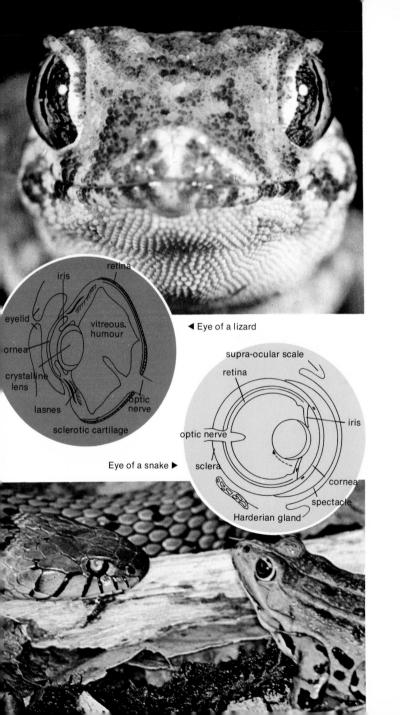

iris

retina

eyelid

vitreous
humour

ornea

crystalline
lens

lasnes

optic
nerve

sclerotic cartilage

◀ Eye of a lizard

supra-ocular scale

retina

iris

optic nerve

sclera

cornea

spectacle

Harderian gland

Eye of a snake ▶

the eyeball. Thus an object is brought into focus by the superposition of the four images. As far as the eyes of the Gekkonidae are concerned, most species have the 'spectacle' formed by the merger of the eyelids. The only members of this family with movable eyelids are the Old World geckos.

Another interesting family of Saurians from the point of view of the formation of the eyes is the Chamaeleontidae. Here the eyes are large, protruding, and almost completely covered by a wide, single eyelid which is in turn covered with tiny scales, with a hole left for the pupil. They are extremely mobile, and can swivel through an angle of 180°

▲ The eye of a chameleon   ▲ The eye of a gecko

in relation to the direction of the animal's head.

In addition each eye can move independently of the other. So, while one eye looks forward, the other can be swivelled round for a explorative glance to detect, at any given moment, a possible prey without the latter being aware of this manoeuvre.

In the subterranean species the eyes are always very small. Some cases even show a complete atrophy of these organs, as in the case of the Dibamidae among the Saurians, and the blind burrowing snakes among the Serpentes. The eye is often protected by reinforced and not very mobile eyelids. In

172

other instances we find a transparent 'window' corresponding to the lower eyelid. Lastly, some animals have a scale which is especially thin and semi-transparent, and therefore allows partial vision. As well as being related to the animal's eyesight, these structures also have the additional task of protecting the delicate visual organs from particles of earth and other dirt which these creatures inevitably come across during their life as burrowers. Various experiments to do with the eyesight of reptiles have been carried out on rattle-snakes. The results have shown that these vipers (although the argument can undoubtedly be

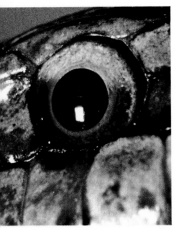

▲ The eye of the smooth snake *Coronella austriaca*

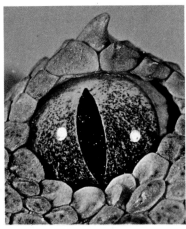

▲ The eye of a horned asp *Cerastes cerastes*

extended to all animals with eyes of the same size) can see moving objects at a distance of 450 metres.

A feature peculiar to certain Saurians (Scincidae and Agamidae) and especially to the tuatara, is the presence on top of the head of the so-called pineal organ or 'third eye' which is linked to the brain.

Some researchers believe that this organ may have a sensory function, for instance in the tuatara acting as a light meter, while in lizards it may control temperature.

In general, in relation to each eye, the reptiles have two large lachrymal glands which emit secretions. These 'tears' may or may not be carried along in lachrymal canaliculi which open both outwards and inwards, in the upper part of the nose. The copious 'tears' shed by nesting sea turtles are actually the products of the salt glands which are located alongside the eyes.

The structure and development of the organ of hearing varies considerably within the class. However there is usually an eardrum which is closed off by the tympanic membrane. Inside, the eardrum communicates with the pharynx by means of a duct called the Eustachian tube. The middle ear has just one bone, the columella, which communicates directly with the inner ear. The tortoises and turtles have a remarkable sensitivity to vibrations throughout their bodies.

The crocodiles are the only animals which have a kind of outer ear with a mobile pavilion and a small auricular aperture which is shut off by a flap of skin when submerged.

Snakes can only pick up low frequency airborne vibrations, but it is thought that they can receive other vibrations through the ground by means of their facial bones.

In the burrowing species, such as some members of the Scincidae, the tympanum or middle ear is situated quite deep, and in many cases the duct linking the middle ear with the outside is closed to prevent particles of earth damaging the delicate structures of this organ. In the Dibamidae even the auricular aperture is totally absent.

The sense of taste does not appear to be very developed in any of the members of this class, evidently because it is of little importance for them. It is situated on the tongue, and its function (at least in certain Saurians and in snakes) is nevertheless connected with the sense of smell and touch. The Helodermatidae, the only venomous Saurians, go in search of food using almost exclusively their sense of taste, although they probably use their sense of smell too. When a heloderm (*Heloderma*) follows a smell, it shoots out its tongue at intervals, almost as if it were sampling the ground. The tongue is just a means of conveying smell-containing particles to two special cavities in the palate.

Similarly, Old World monitor lizards (*Varanus*), New World teids, and the Bornean *Lanthanotus* or 'earless monitor' (a rare Saurian whose internal structure exhibits features that were once thought to be the precursor of the snakes), have a tongue that can be evaginated and retracted just like the tongue of a snake.

Smells and scents are, on the whole, received by the nasal fossae. In the Squamata and Rhynchocephalia, in particular, it is the Jacobson's organ which undertakes this task.

Additional sensory structures take the form of dot-like elements which occur on various scales on the head and body of many reptiles. Their function seems to be connected with stimuli of a tactile nature.

In the families Boidae and Viperidae there are facial pits. These are cavities divided into two superposed chambers by a crosswise membrane, slightly deeper than the actual surface of the face itself. In the pit vipers they are situated between the nostril and the eye while in those boids in which pits occur they lie on or at the side of the scales on the upper lip. They are sensitive to infra-red radiation and their function would therefore be heat receptors enabling the snakes to locate warm, in other words live, prey, and particularly useful to nocturnal species which hunt by night.

Preservation of the species

Of all the features peculiar to the class of reptiles, the most essential to the success achieved by these creatures in the course of their history has been the amniotic egg. This meant the end of the type of external fertilization as used by fishes and amphibians, and lead to internal fertilization carried out by copulatory organs which anticipated those present much later in the mammals.

▼ Malayan monitor lizard *Varanus salvator*

175

▼ Grass snake *Natrix natrix*

▼ Desert monitor *Varanus griseus*

176

With the exception of the tuatara, all male reptiles have a copulatory organ at the base of their tail which is usually kept introflexed or invaginated, and is only evaginated through the cloacal aperture during the actual act of copulation. In the tuatara, on the other hand, mating together with the introduction of the male sperm in to the female's cloaca takes place simply by the proper positioning of the genital orifices.

In the Saurians and Ophidia, the copulatory organ is formed by two hollow formations, the hemipenes, which can be used at will, but always only one at a time. In the various members of the class, the time which elapses between fertilization and egg-laying varies: in some cases it is quite short (just a few hours), and in others it may be a matter of years. The longest gap applies to the cat-eyed snake (*Leptodeira annulata*) of tropical America (five years) and the diamond-back terrapin (*Malaclemys*) found in the southern United States (four years).

Among the Saurians, particularly in the species *Lacerta saxicola*, and in certain species of Teiidae belonging to the genus *Cnemidophorus* (race-runners), it would seem that unisexual populations occur and reproduction without sexual union takes place (parthenogenesis) and further individuals are produced from unfertilized eggs.

The most prolific reptiles are probably the large sea turtles which can, on average, lay up to 100 eggs at a time: the green turtle can lay up to 200 eggs, and the loggerhead lays between 60 and 150 eggs each time. On the contrary, the *Malacochersus tornieri* (the pancake tortoise), which is still in the same Order, is a soft-shelled tortoise which lays just one egg at a time.

The crocodiles and pythons are also fairly prolific: between 15 and 88 eggs for the American alligator, between 25 and 95 eggs for the Nile crocodile, and 100 or more eggs in the case of the Indian python and the reticulate python.

The Saurians however are somewhat less prolific, with the exception of the monitor lizards, which lay between 30 and 60 eggs at a time. Most Saurians lay an average of 2–15 eggs each season. Even though most species are oviparous, there are cases of ovoviviparity and viviparity among the Saurians and snakes in particular.

In the first case, eggs are produced which open a few seconds before being laid; in the second case live young are delivered which resemble adults and are completely independent and self-sufficient. There are no instances of metamorphosis in the class of reptiles. Viviparity may possibly be associated with the impossibility of incubating eggs in regions which have a cold climate. The common lizard (*Lacerta vivipara*) is a classic example of this. In regions situated at more extreme latitudes, where the short summers do not permit eggs to develop and hatch, this lizard retains them in its own body throughout the period of incubation, and gives birth to live young lizards.

In more southerly regions with a more temperate climate, the females of this same species are oviparous.

The commonest examples of viviparity are to be found in the family Scincidae and the family Lacertidae, among the Saurians, and in the Boidae and Viperidae among the snakes.

▼ Freshwater terrapins genus *Malaclemys*; the smaller one is the male

A new egg

The egg is laid already fertilized, protected by a solid lining which is equipped for the development of the embryo.

Compared with the eggs of amphibians and fishes, the reptilian egg has many special features. At the centre is the embryo, joined to the yolk-sac by the funiculus, which is known as the umbilical peduncle because it is attached to the embryo's umbilicus. The yolk-sac represents the main food reserve for the embryo during its development.

The embryo itself is enveloped by the amniotic sac, full of amniotic fluid which keeps it wet and protects it from blows and jolts. The whole thing is, in turn, enclosed in a third sac, called the allantois. As the embryo grows, the yolk becomes considerably smaller, and the allantois increases in size so as

▼ Giant tortoises mating

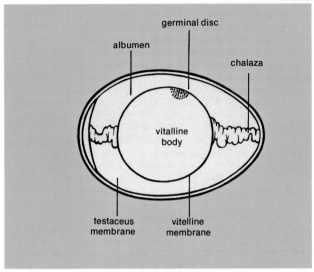

▲ Cross-section of a lizard's egg

to be better able to carry out its two functions: the collection of waste produced by the embryo's metabolism – this consists mainly of uric acid and ammoniac compounds – and the regulation of the movement of incoming respiratory gases, such as oxygen, and outgoing carbon dioxide.

In addition to the allantois, and working our way outwards, there is a thin membrane called the chorion, which is attached to the shell and has a protective function.

In the turtles and tortoises, and in the crocodiles, the chorion has a supplementary nutritive function, and contains the reserve albumen.

The embryo is fed via the blood. The tight network of blood vessels which surrounds the entire surface of the yolk-sac absorbs the necessary nutritive substances, and conveys them as far as the abdominal region of the embryo which, in this way, receives as much as it needs to grow and become formed. The embryo breathes through the pores in the egg-shell, which permit the inflow of atmospheric oxygen and the outflow of carbon dioxide produced as waste by the respiratory system. This movement of gas to the tissues of the embryo is handled, in order, by first the haemoglobin molecules of the red corpuscles circulating in the

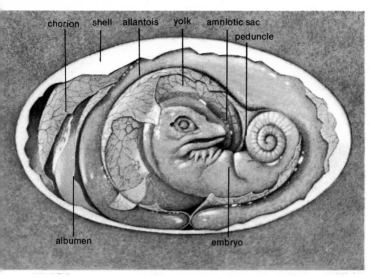

chorion shell allantois yolk amniotic sac
peduncle

albumen   embryo

▲ An alligator's egg showing developing embryo within the yolk-sac

tiny capillaries of the chorion, then by those contained in
the thin capillaries of the allantois, which in turn are
directly connected to the blood vessels of the embryo.

From the point of view of dimensions, the largest recorded
egg of any reptile was that laid by a long-necked quadruped
dinosaur which lived towards the end of the Cretaceous Era:
the so-called *Hypselosaurus*. The fossil egg discovered
measured 33 cm in length. Conversely, the smallest egg
belongs to a present-day reptile, the *Sphaerodactylus
macrolepsis*, a geckonid found in the Antilles which, as an
adult, measures just 5 cm in length, and consequently lays an
egg just 6 mm long.

In shape the eggs may also vary greatly. In the sea turtles
and certain species of freshwater terrapins, they are
generally spherical. In most other cases they are ovoid, or
egg-shaped. The colour is varied, but is usually brown,
yellow, or pure white. In some cases they may be speckled,
and this can be taken as a form of defensive chromatic
mimeticism designed to conceal the eggs from the prying
eyes of possible predators.

The consistency of the shell also differs from species to
species, depending on the degree of calcification. Turtles and

tortoises, crocodiles and Gekkonidae – the last being the only such case among the Squamata – have hard, fragile eggs, like birds' eggs. Under the microscope the shell appears to be formed of a series of fibrous layers which are regularly superposed at right angles, and impregnated with calcium salts in varying degrees.

In certain other turtles and tortoises, the eggs have a soft, rubbery consistency, because of the incomplete calcification of the whole shell. Saurians (except the Gekkonidae) and snakes tend to have parchment-like eggs, and are in fact often deformed by contact with harder solid objects.

Sometimes, and this applies to the Gekkonidae, they are not laid with the final consistency, but harden once they come in contact with the air. Lastly, in some instances the eggs are held together by a sticky substance which permits the formation of clusters or else attaches the eggs to stones or cracks in rocks.

Once the development of the embryo is complete, after the incubation period, the new animal formed in the egg must be able to break out of the tough shell, which has by now become too small for its increased size. The embryos of the Serpentes and Saurians actually have a small very sharp tooth inserted on the tip of the premaxillary bone, and, in oviparous species, this is bent forwards. This enables them to break the shell. In the embryos of turtles, tortoises and crocodiles this same function is carried out by the horny caruncle at the tip of the snout.

Egg-teeth and caruncles are, however, structures which drop off quite quickly, within a day in the case of an egg tooth, and up to four weeks in the case of a caruncle.

Here again the Gekkonidae are different. They are in fact the only reptiles with two egg-teeth, positioned beside each other, which work simultaneously.

In the case of the viviparous species, the structure of the egg undergoes certain modifications in relation with the differing type of reproduction. In particular, the shell becomes much thinner, and in some cases is reduced to a tiny covering, while in other animals it disappears altogether.

Among the chameleons there are species which have adopted this latter type of reproduction. It is thought that this particular feature safeguards the eggs by reducing the risk of them falling to the ground as they are being laid. The whole reproductive process is brought to completion while the mother is perched in a tree and when the newborn animals emerge from their mother they are enveloped in a

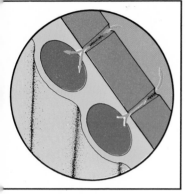

▲ The embryo breathes
through the pores in the shell

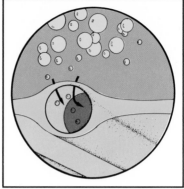

▲ The embryo feeds by means
of the blood vessels

sticky membrane which gives them a hold on the branch.
They may escape from this thin membrane almost
immediately, or remain confined for some time.

Again among the Saurians, certain Gekkonidae are
viviparous (the genera *Hoplodactylus* and *Naultinus*), as are
certain Iguanidae (genus *Phrynosoma*), the slow-worm, and
one species of alligator lizard, among the Anguidae.

▼ Extra-embryonic membrane of a reptile in the final stage of its development

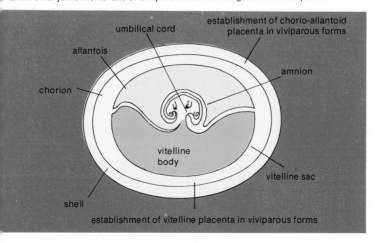

▲ A North American racer snake (*Coluber*) with her eggs

A sea-turtle laying her eggs ▶

Most sea-snakes are viviparous but one genus (*Laticauda*) returns to land to lay eggs. There are several advantages of viviparity compared with the more traditional oviparous method. First and foremost the mother unintentionally selects for herself, and thus for the young developing inside her, the most suitable temperatures. Secondly, by being inside the body of a parent the eggs are well protected, and are less exposed to the dangers posed by possible predators, and attacks from parasites (certain fungi infest eggs), or sudden and harmful climatic changes or dehydration.

▲ Common lizards *Lacerta vivipara*

Development and growth

Given that reptiles' eggs belong to the category which
comparative anatomy defines as polar or telolecithal, the
initial phases of their development generally take the form
of a series of successive divisions known as the
segmentations.

These segmentations give rise to the germinal disc (or
blastodisc) of the embryo. From this mass of initial cells, and
by means of a whole series of processes including not only
segmentation but also an invagination of the cells, the
primitive embryonic or germ layers start to take shape: the
endoderm, from which the digestive apparatus and its
appendages is formed; towards the outside, the ectoderm,
from which after just eight hours incubation the primitive
lines are formed which will eventually represent the spinal
cord; and the mesoderm, which also partly develops from
the primitive line and gives rise to the skeleton, musculature,
blood vessels, and excretory and reproductive organs. The
ectoderm, on the other hand, forms the integuments, the
nervous system and the sense organs attached to it. In
addition there are the embryonic appendages (chorion,
amnion, yolk-sac and allantois). The amnion is formed from

186

a fold of the extra-embryonic area which surrounds the embryo. At a certain moment the two lateral amniotic folds merge, along the margins, and as a result two membranes are formed. One is in direct contact with the embryo (also known as the amnion), and the other outside it – the chorion. The vitelline sac then forms following the growth of the extra-embryonic area around the vitellin.

When they emerge from their eggs, young reptiles are identical to the adults of the same species. The smallest reptiles grow fastest: the common lizard grows in just one year from 37–47 mm to 108 mm, including the tail; certain African Agamidae double their length in the first six months after birth. In the reptiles, sexual maturity is linked more with an animal's size than it's age. Some New World chameleons can reproduce a year after hatching, but certain small Lacertidae take two years to reach the same stage. Snakes are sexually mature between 2 and 5 years, and the crocodiles, followed by the tuatara, are the last to develop.

▼ An asp-viper (*Vipera aspis*) giving birth

Behaviour

It should be pointed out, to begin with, that the study of the behaviour of reptiles in the extremely varied habitats in which they live, has been associated, in a great many cases, with research carried out on subjects being held in captivity, or, on subjects which have been singled out so that they can be kept under supervision.

As for any other member of the animal kingdom, the whole existence of reptiles hinges on two fundamental factors: reproduction, to ensure the continued existence of the species; and individual survival, which is made more difficult due to the fact that, as parents, this class does not display much concern for the care of the young they bring into the world.

Bearing these two essential factors in mind, the most interesting behavioural features of the various reptiles are discussed in this chapter.

The first problem related to the continued existence of the

species is that of being able to meet and then recognize the right partner or mate. This means a member of the same species, but of the opposite sex. Where reptiles are concerned this is not as straightforward as it may be for other classes of animals, because, in general, the differences in secondary sexual features are slight.

In this class, there is also a unique and curious instance of hermaphroditism in a snake belonging to the Viperidae, living in certain Brazilian islands. In the *Bothrops insularis*, the male and female sex organs appear simultaneously.

As a general rule males differ from their mates in size, colour, shape of head and shape and length of tail. Sometimes, and this applies to the Saurians above all, the males display brightly coloured cutaneous formations during the mating season. Of all the orders, the Testudines show the greatest difference in size between males and females.

▲ Adders (*Vipera berus*) courti

▲ Cuban anole *Anolis equestris*

Contrary to the usual pattern, the females are far larger than the males, and this is very evident in certain freshwater terrapins, such as *Malaclemys* or diamond-back terrapins, and the painted terrapins, where the females have carapaces which may be as much as twice the length of the males.

The opposite is true of the crocodiles, however, where the males are considerably larger than the females, as is the case for the Saurians (with the exception of the slow-worms and possibly a few other species of snake-like Saurians) and the Rhynchocephalia. In the case of the snakes the rôles are reversed: female pythons, for example, can be as much as 1.8 m longer than males, whose average length is 4.5 m.

There are very few morphological differences: almost all male animals have a stronger skull, a longer tail, and paired swellings at the tail base due to the presence of the copulatory organ.

▲ Male sea iguanas (*Amblyrhynchus cristatus*) fighting

Only the Saurians show crests on the back and/or tail, and horns and cutaneous appendages in males. Still referring to this group, the large males of the genera *Lacerta* and *Tupinambis* have markedly hypertrophic jaw muscles. The femoral pores are also a feature peculiar to males.

The only genus of snake which has a feature of sexual differentiation is the *Langaha*, a Madagascan tree snake which has a strange conical facial appendage that differs in shape in the sexes. In the Boidae and in three other groups of primitive snakes, the rudiments of the femur projects as a horny spur at the side of the cloaca. The males of some boas

192

and pythons use this spur or claw to stimulate the female during courtship.

Male lizards, and many male Agamidae and Iguanidae, generally have brighter colour-schemes, and during the mating season, often display shades of red, yellow, blue and orange.

Coloration may also change with sexual maturity and there are numerous examples of such entogenetic colour change.

▲ The Galapagos sea iguana

Territorial and courtship displays
In many members of the class of reptiles, mating is preceded by various types of display which generally have the dual purpose of winning a female and defending a certain territorial area from intruders of the same species.

Among tortoises and turtles, courting is often characterized by a kind of pursuit by the males: the box terrapins belonging to the genus *Terrapene* let themselves be nipped along the edges of their carapace by their future mate, as well as on the head and neck, when they have been pursued for some time; the male giant Galapagos tortoise rhythmically sways its head up and down, in a similar way to certain Saurians, when they invite a female to mate. Among the aquatic species, both marine and freshwater, a strange parade occurs in the water in which, having once selected the female, the male confronts her and beats his flippers together in such a way that the claws vibrate close to the female's head. Thus stimulated, she in turn moves towards the male, forcing him to retreat. After this dance has lasted a while, the female plunges and situates herself below the male, who then fertilizes her. In this order the males are often obliged to fertilize the females in an almost vertical position because of their large cumbersome carapace. The toes on the hind-legs, or the horny scales with which these are often equipped, give a tighter and safer grip during copulation, which may last for several hours in some cases.

Not very much is known about the mating habits of crocodiles in general. Copulation occurs at night, and at this stage of life, the males become particularly fierce and aggressive, and can emit dull sounds, not unlike mooing, to summon their mate, while at the same time keeping any dangerous rival at a safe distance.

▼ Combat dances of male snakes

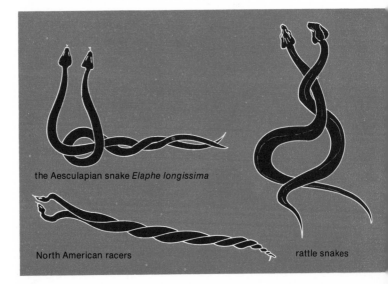

the Aesculapian snake *Elaphe longissima*

North American racers

rattle snakes

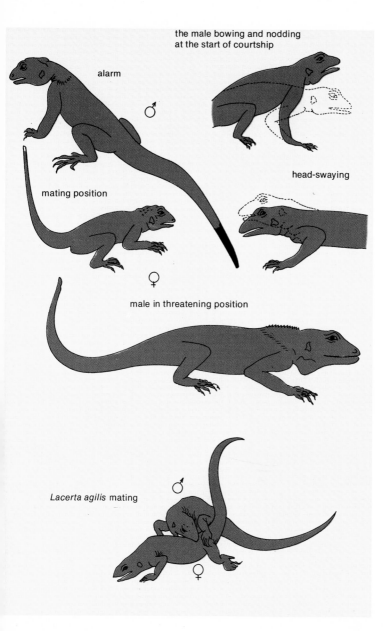

the male bowing and nodding
at the start of courtship

alarm

♂

head-swaying

mating position

♀

male in threatening position

Lacerta agilis mating

♂

♀

▲ Types of behaviour in the Saurians

195

Among the Saurians, the Agamidae and certain Iguanidae show extreme territorial and nuptial forms of behaviour, in which intimidation is the essential ingredient. The ritual is usually quite stereotyped, and in fact an agamid considers mating as something akin to a fight. When he has singled out a female, he places himself beside her, presenting a larger surface by stretching his brightly coloured skin.

Then, as happens when a fight begins, he moves his head up and down, drawing closer to the female step by step, until he is close enough to seize her by the neck with his jaws. At this point, he hooks the ends of his legs around her back and twines the hindmost part of his body under the female's body. She, in turn, bends her tail upwards, so as to allow the sexual orifices to link up, and mating then takes place, usually lasting no longer than a couple of minutes.

The iguanas display similar intimidatory techniques when faced with rivals intruding upon their chosen territory.

The various threatening attitudes (such as rocking and flattening the head, making the crest bristle, and puffing out the throat) are accompanied by a use of colour. In many cases, these animals have very bright colorations, usually red or orange, on the skin, concealed between the throat-scales. The snakes resort to an equally varied and elaborate series of sexual techniques. In fact the males of many species, before winning the female, often display their prowess with rivals of the same sex by ritual 'dances'. Rattle-snakes and vipers, the highly venomous mambas among the cobras and varied species of Colubridae tightly intertwine their entire bodies, and engage in a sort of slow swaying dance. Male boas and pythons stimulate the females by using their rudimentary femoral bones to scratch the flanks of the female. Certain experiments have shown that during this period the sense of smell becomes particularly acute, possibly to make it easier to identify the partner at a distance or by night.

Polygamy is common in almost every member of this class. It is believed that one of the few monogamous reptiles is the extremely venomous Asiatic (spectacled) cobra.

Nesting and care of the young

In general reptiles lay their eggs in sand or soil, beneath a pile of pebbles or leaves. They usually look for a slightly depressed hollow or a natural hole which acts as a nest. Reptiles are not in the habit of building nests or of looking after their young, but there are exceptions to this rule.

The sea turtles are perhaps the most concerned of all about the fate of their offspring. After fertilization they lay their eggs in holes dug in sandy beaches on which they land after travelling vast distances through the ocean, often in large groups. Considering their large bulk this is quite an amazing accomplishment.

Once the eggs have been laid, the turtles fill in the holes with sand, and try to smooth off the surface to protect the nest from predators.

Depending on the species crocodilians lay their eggs either in an excavated hole or on a mound of vegetation. Hole nesting is believed to be more primitive and is practised by the gharial, false gharial and many of the crocodiles while the alligators and caimans are mound nesters.

Unlike many reptiles which leave their young to fend for themselves, the females of some crocodilians remain near the nest throughout the incubation period. When the eggs

Caribbean sea turtles are able to travel large distances from their feeding grounds to the breeding grounds

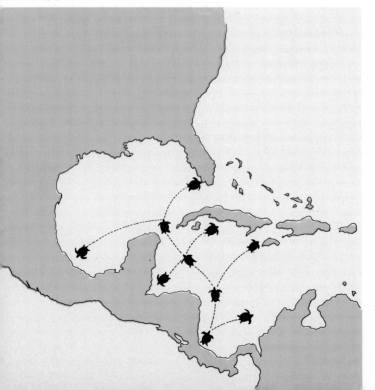

hatch, the young call out to the mother with a squeak-like cry for help.

Similarly, the tuatara lays her 5–15 eggs in shallow holes which are dug in the ground near the den. The eggs remain here for between 13 and 15 months before hatching, this being the longest incubation period of all reptiles.

Few lizards and snakes build nests but the Bengal monitor lizard, the *Chamaeleo dilepis*, certain skinks and certain Anguidae, dig a kind of incubation chamber like those prepared by turtles, where the eggs are laid. Similarly the hamadryad or king cobra builds a mound of leaves in which she lays her eggs and which she guards until the eggs hatch.

Certain Scincidae and certain Anguidae brood their eggs by lying on them. The female of American *Eumeces*, like the female American alligator, looks after her young especially at the moment of hatching, helping them to emerge from the shell and guiding them through their first days in the outside world. It would even seem that she personally attends to the daily hygiene of her young, by licking them every so often like a cat.

Where the snakes are concerned, the female Indian python is known to brood her eggs and assist in their incubation by raising the temperature of her body. There is however some doubt attached to most other reports of brooding by snakes, and parental care seems to be generally lacking in snakes.

In the viviparous forms, be it Saurian or snake, there is total indifference on the part of the parents, or rather of the mother, towards her offspring. Among the Saurians only one skink (*Mabuya trivittata*) and one member of the Lacertidae, the night lizard (*Xantusia vigilis*) show some concern for their newborn young, by helping them extricate themselves from the embryonic membranes.

Survival

In the case of the reptiles, the equipment designed for survival has, essentially, two functions: to avoid being caught by some other larger and stronger predator; and to try, without being seen if possible, to catch prey.

Mimetic colours and techniques of disguise, threatening postures, the emission of harmful substances, voluntary amputation, and the secretion of venom are all part of the defence mechanisms with which reptiles are endowed.

The fact that the body colour may blend with the animal's

The common chameleon *Chamaeleo chamaeleon* 199

▲ Papuan tree-python *Chondropython viridis*

▲ European gecko *Phyllodactylus europaeus*

environment represents the first and most common form of mimeticism used for defence in this class. The crocodiles and many freshwater terrapins and tortoises have a camouflaging coloration whereby their greenish-brown bodies matches the predominant colour of the surrounding vegetation. The green coloration which is so common in arboreal lizards and snakes has a similar significance. In many cases the colour of the back is darker, and the belly lighter. This applies particularly to the aquatic species which have the dual problem of concealing themselves not only from the eye of enemies living at a greater depth than they, but also enemies living nearer the surface, on dry land, or in the air. Many members of this class have a non-uniform coloration, where light-coloured areas alternate with more sober colours. This arrangement provides a perfect answer to the need for defensive mimeticism. In terrapins belonging to the genus *Chrysemys* (painted terrapins) even the eye is concealed by a series of yellowish stripes which run across the eyelid and iris, and thus provide the animal with an even better camouflage.

It is commonly believed that of all the reptiles the chameleons can best adapt their coloration to the colours about them. However, it has been possible to show that the mimicry of chameleons is an indirect form of mimicry. In other words, when they are relaxed, in optimum light and temperature conditions in relation to their requirements, these creatures assume the colours which enable them to blend in with their surroundings, not so much for defensive reasons, but rather to give them the chance to attack a prey, unseen. Thus the colour changes for which chameleons are famed are in response to alterations in temperature and light as well as to their emotional state and not as generally believed merely in order to match their background.

Colour changes are produced by the activity of special cells (chromatophores), which contain granules of different colour pigments and, depending on the nervous stimulus reaching them, may be selectively contracted or expanded. In many cases the effect of a mimetic coloration is made even more effective by the position in which reptiles manage to place their bodies. By flattening their bodies and gently swaying the chameleons can make themselves look like leaves fluttering in the breeze; the tree-snakes of the genera *Oxybellis*, *Thelotornis* and *Ahaetulla* are notorious for their perfect resemblance to lianas; some arboreal geckos merge perfectly with the bark of the trees in which they live, both because of their mimetic coloration and because of the shape of their bodies. Among the venomous snakes, and more particularly the Elapidae (such as cobras), there are the notorious coral-snakes which live in the tropical regions of the Americas. They are so-called because of the dominant coloration of their skin and commonly have a series of red, black and yellow rings, which alternate in different ways in the various species.

Curiously enough both harmless as well as mildly venomous species that look very much the same as their more fearsome colleagues live in the same regions as the latter. This is obviously a case of protective mimicry whereby the resemblance to the venomous forms afford them a measure of protection.

The defensive devices available to the reptiles can be divided into two groups: actual weapons, and psychological weapons. This latter category includes all those attitudes, such as body positions, intimidating expressions, feigned death, by which these animals try to prevent their enemies from attacking.

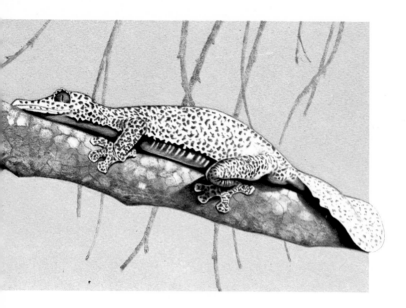

▲ Leaf-tailed gecko *Uroplates fimbriatus*

The tortoises and turtles are undoubtedly the least well-equipped order in this respect. Apart from their tough beak, they have no other specific structure for defence, and simply rely on their strong carapace and even, in some species, on withdrawing their head and neck in the event of an attack.

The fiercest of all in the face of an attacker is the freshwater snapping turtle (*Macrochelys temmincki*) found in the United States. Its warrior-like spirit is helped by its remarkable agility, which singles it out from its fellow turtles in other species.

The crocodiles have always been stronger and fiercer than the other creatures sharing their habitat, and in fact only need to strike aggressive attitudes or use their additional weapons of defence on rare occasions. Even when they are motionless with their jaws fully agape, this is not meant to frighten nearby animals, but simply regulates their body-temperature by increasing ventilation. It also enables certain birds, with which they have established a relationship of mutual collaboration, to hop into their mouth and eat the leeches clinging to the palate and gums.

Lizards and snakes, on the other hand, have a wide variety of threatening displays, in addition to various modifications designed to discourage their predators.

The strong tailed monitor lizards and certain Agamidae with their tails covered with hard, pointed, large scales, arranged in spiny verticils, rely on this type of defence as soon as they are under attack.

Certain Cordylidae, such as the famous African 'girdle-tailed' lizards, vigorously shake their armoured tails when confronted by snakes, their traditional enemies, and this type of defence seems to be successful.

The group of weapons derived from specialized epidermal structures includes the spiny protuberances found in the horned 'toads' (more accurately, lizards) living in the hot desert regions of the United States. Similarly, the spiny layer covering the upper part of the head, the trunk and the tail of the Australian thorny devil (*Moloch horridus*), and the facial horns found in certain chameleons are all designed to frighten off their enemies.

Where the snakes are concerned, one of the most effective warning mechanisms is the rattle-snake's rattle. This warning device, which resembles the whirring rattle, prompts the victims of these snakes to take immediate flight.

▼ The bearded lizard *Amphibolurus barbatus*

The Australian frilled lizard (*Clamydosaurus kingi*),
is perhaps one of the most spectacular creatures
where this type of intimidatory attitude is concerned. The
head is tipped upwards, with the mouth held wide open to
show the bright red mucous membrane lining. This is
accompanied by violent puffing and nervous movements of
the tail. However, the most striking and important part of
this display of force, which is unique in the genus, is the
unfolding of the neck frill to a width of some 25 cm. The
neck frill appears to be specifically designed to increase the
animal's size to terrifying proportions and make it appear far

◀ Frilled lizard *Clamydosaurus kingi*

▲ The defensive position of the desert monitor *Varanus griseus*

larger than the average length of 20 cm for this Saurian. The
'beard' present on the throat of the bearded lizard has the
same function, as have the banner-like appendages on the
head of the *Phrynocephalus*, which also turn reddish in
colour when erect.

The tactic of appearing larger than life is also a typical
device used by certain Iguanidae: face to face with a snake,
their traditional enemy, the crested *Corythophanes cristatus*,
a Central American iguana, uses the effect of its profile, by
flattening its body and rearing up on its hind legs to make it
appear taller; other Saurians, such as the monitor lizards, for
example, react to enemies by raising the foremost part of the
body, swelling the neck and beating the tail as if it were a
whip ready to lash the foe.

This type of intimidatory attitude is also quite common

▲ Stoddart's horned agama *Ceratophora stoddarti*

among the snakes. Of all the snakes, however, the species in which this phenomenon becomes truly impressive is the black and yellow Guyana chicken-snake (*Spilotes pullatus*) found in South America, which can puff out its neck into a large egg shape. Such threatening or defensive postures may also be accompanied by the display of bright coloration on the skin of the neck between the scales as for example in the tropical African boomslang and the African bird-eating or twig snakes.

One of the best-known threatening postures is that used by the extremely venomous cobras. These animals can dilate their necks, and at the same time raise the foremost section of their trunk into the air. This dilatation is made possible by the unusual length and mobility of the cervical ribs in these species: these move upwards, stretching the skin of the neck and thus producing the hood, which is either pear-shaped or fairly oval in shape. In addition, the hood has distinctively shaped patches on the back. These are either stellate (star-shaped) or roundish.

Some Colubridae also imitate the cobras. Members of the genus *Ptyas*, for example, puff out their neck if threatened, raise the front section of the trunk and huff vigorously while rocking their body at the same time.

Another typical intimidatory position used by quite a large number of snake species is the one peculiar to venomous and non-venomous species in which the ventral areas of the body become brightly coloured and where the tail closely resembles the head in shape and coloration. When a snake with these morphological features is bothered, it hides its head under the coils of its body and lets the tail, which is held upright, sway to and fro slightly, in order to catch the attacker's eye. The hog-nosed snakes (*Heterodon*), very large North American Colubridae, are also very skilful fakers. As soon as they feel threatened they put on an amazing act: first they puff themselves up, assuming a threatening attitude, tail quivering and hissing powerfully. If this ploy is unsuccessful, they feign death by turning over on to their back, opening their mouth wide, and even spitting blood in some instances. They then remain motionless in this position, simply waiting for the outcome of their charade.

The defensive positions used by certain Saurians, such as the South African girdle-tailed lizard (*Cordylus cataphractus*) and the North American alligator lizards,

▼ Defensive positions of Saurians

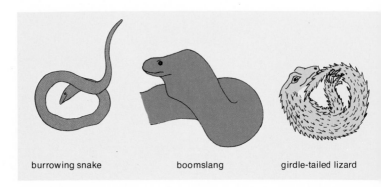

burrowing snake · · · · · · · · · · boomslang · · · · · · · · · · girdle-tailed lizard

▲ Faced with danger, the hog-nosed snake feigns death ▼

▲ Horned rattle snake *Crotalus cerastes*

deserve to be mentioned. In both cases the animals try to make themselves smaller and protect the ventral areas of their bodies, which are more vulnerable because they house important organs. At the slightest hint of danger the former (*C. cataphractus*) takes refuge in a crack in a rock and bends its tail, which is fairly long, until the danger has passed. The alligator lizards use a similar but even more pronounced technique, by gripping their tails in their jaws, while the body wraps itself around a small branch.

If threatened, the plated lizards lie prostrate on the ground with their legs lying alongside their body, and resist any attempt to turn them over on to their back, thus exposing the belly. The layer of spiny, bony scales helps this defensive tactic.

Within the family Lacertidae – still in the order of Saurians – one finds the least number of defensive mechanisms. In fact these animals do not change colour in response to specific moods, nor do they have protective or intimidatory formations. Also they do not hiss or produce venomous substances. However, when they do engage in battle they fight ferociously to the bitter end, with violent bites which often cause fatal wounds in the enemy.

The Saurians include few species which make sounds. One of the best-known, however, belongs to the Gekkonidae and the genus *Teratoscincus*, found in the deserts of Persia and Pakistan. If disturbed, this animal produces a distinctive noise by rubbing together the wide scales on the top of the tail. This capacity applies not only to the original tail but if

▲ *Oligodon taeniatus* presents an attacker with the bright-red underside of its tail

voluntarily amputated, also exists in the new-grown tail.

Among the Viperidae, the saw-scaled viper (*Echis carinata*) has, as its name implies, serrated ridges on its body scales. By coiling itself into a tight spiral it can rub its body coils against these ridges and produce a grating sound. The egg-eating snakes (Dasypeltinae) do the same and although harmless, they have a marked resemblance to the dangerously venomous saw-scaled viper. Of all the sounds emitted, the most typical where the reptiles are concerned is the ability to hiss: tortoises, turtles, alligators, monitor lizards, chameleons, snakes venomous and otherwise, all use this method to intimidate their enemies. The mechanism usually involves the inhalation of a large quantity of air, which is then violently expelled through the mouth and the nostrils.

One of the most feared sound instruments is the rattle of the Crotalinae. The vibrations produce a distinctive whirring sound, which is an alarm signal which enables the rattler to keep large animals, with whom a fight might damage both parties, at a safe distance. The whirring sound of the rattle can be heard 20 metres away. Certain small species of rattlesnake, for example the *Sistrurus miliaris*, produce a

▲ Grass snake taking refuge in water

more subtle whirring sound, which can only be heard 2 or 3 metres away. The effectiveness of this device is dependent not only on the mood of the snake in question, but also on the physical conditions of the environment: it is of course completely dulled in water and muffled in humid conditions. In a hot, dry climate, on the other hand, it becomes louder in tone.

Another warning device is that used by an American or Sonora coral-snake, the *Micruroides euryxanthus*, and a harmless colubrid, the *Gyalopium canum*. Both these species are capable of making their presence known by emitting dry-sounding and repeated noises from the cloacal aperture, produced by the expulsion of air.

Many members of the animal kingdom can emit substances which have an irritant action on possible attackers. One of the best-known Saurians which has adopted this defence method is the horned toad or lizard, found in the deserts of North America. If bothered, this small Saurian squirts blood in its enemy's face from its eyes. Herpetologists have interpreted this phenomenon as a direct consequence of the swelling undergone by the animal's entire body to appear threatening: the nictitating membrane, which is very thin, clearly cannot support this excessive

▼ Black-necked cobra *Naja nigricollis*

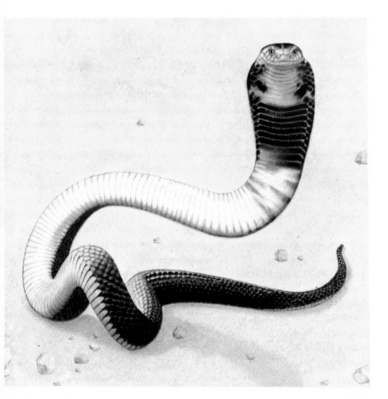

strain and its capillaries burst, thus causing the violent outflow of blood.

Some Gekkonidae, however, emit from special tubercles situated on the tail (or from the actual tail skin) a viscous, sticky substance which is aimed directly from the tail at the enemy's face, up to about 30 cm away. As the tail is their main instrument of defence, these Saurians are much less ready to lose them, and less able to regrow them.

Apart from the use of venom, many snakes also use chemical substances as weapons to safeguard their well-being. For instance, the wood snakes belonging to the genus *Tropidophis* (family Boidae) spit blood when attacked; certain Colubridae emit irritant substances from their nuchal-dorsal glands. These substances then impregnate the skin of the back, thus making them unpleasant to catch, because they have an irritant action on the mucous membrane in the attacker's mouth.

Lastly, other Colubridae and certain Viperidae produce vile substances in the anal glands situated at the sides of the cloacal aperture and often emit them together with their faeces, thus confusing the attacker and enabling a hasty retreat.

In some cases they use these same substances to delimit their own territory, scattering them with their tail for a radius of a metre or so.

Muscular strength, for both defence and attack (to overcome a prey for example) is used by the snakes belonging to the Boidae, which includes the boas and the pythons. Because they have no venom, these animals use constriction. Once the enemy has been sighted, the snakes dart upon their prey with lightning speed, and coil themselves around it in such a way as to cause suffocation. It would appear that these snakes are particularly aware of their prey's heartbeat, and only slacken their grip when they are quite sure that the prey is dead. This operation combines both the muscular strength of the trunk, and the numerous sharp teeth which sink into the flesh of the victim, and hold it tight while the creature is being squeezed to death.

As already discussed, some reptiles are characterized by their capacity to voluntarily amputate part of their tail for defensive purposes, so as to divert the attention of an attacker and have time to make good their escape.

Of all the vertebrates, the class of reptiles is certainly the most prolific as far as venomous animals are concerned. With the exception of a few fishes and certain shrews, the

▲ The Malayan pipe-snake *(Cylindrophis rufus)* raises its tail
and hides its head as a defensive measure

venomous vertebrates are as follows: two species of Saurians
belonging to the Helodermatidae, and numerous species of
snakes belonging to the Colubridae, Elapidae, and
Viperidae.

▼ *Thrasops jacksoni* swells its neck when attacked

▼ *Naja naja* in defensive posture. The cervical ribs of the cobra move upwards, stretching the skin of the neck to produce the 'hood'

Despite the fact that traditions and beliefs often refer to venomous Saurians, the only poisonous lizards are the two members of the Helodermatidae, the gila monster (*Heloderma suspectum*) found in the south-western United States and Mexico, and the beaded lizard (*Heloderma horridum*) which is found in western Mexico. They are large, slow-moving and carnivorous, with feet equipped with strong claws used for holding on to their victims (small birds

▲ A green lizard is able to shed its tail when attacked

or mammals), and have short tails.

The major feature of both these species, however, is that they have a powerful venom-apparatus which works most effectively, even though it is not as highly developed and efficient as the type found in the snakes.

The lobed poison glands are confined to the lower jaws. The poison discharges by means of ducts that lead to a mucous fold between the lower lip and the mandible; from

217

there it is believed that it may be drawn up into the series of teeth in the middle of the mandible by capillary action. The teeth in this zone, and usually the fourth and fifth, are grooved and particularly well modified for conducting

▲ A common lizard with a forked tail

venom. In venomous snakes the poison glands and venom injecting apparatus are located in the upper jaw, the glands being situated on each side of the skull and in a few species extending back into the trunk.

The venom of the heloderms contains numerous ingredients which differ from that of the snakes, and in composition possibly resembles only the venom of the cobras. Once bitten, the victim feels an intense pain in the area bitten, and in serious cases may experience paralysis of the respiratory organs. Treatment for a bite from these creatures is similar to that recommended for any kind of venomous bite: seek medical attention.

The procedure of making incisions in and around the site of the bite as a means of releasing some of the injected venom is not recommended because of the danger of introducing bacterial infection. Unfortunately, there is no specific antidote.

Heloderms rarely attack, unless provoked. Herpetologists have often wondered why these animals are venomous. Although they are carnivorous, they in fact feed on eggs, small birds and small rodents, all of which not only put up

▲ A Moorish gecko with its tail newly regrown

little resistance, but are also fairly harmless in terms of their size and stage of development.

The conclusion reached, therefore, is that this weapon is rather a means of personal defence in the face of larger attackers, against whom it would otherwise be hard to rally, because of the lack of adequate body-protection and their slow and sluggish movements. The heloderms are mainly nocturnal creatures, active also in the twilight hours, when the temperature is not too high. Like other animals living in arid regions or deserts, the heloderms are also obliged to put up with fairly marked climatic variations. Thus on the whole their active life is limited to the rainy season between July and September. During dry periods, these animals remain hidden in deep holes which they have dug in the sand, and even give up eating. It is during this period that they make use of the fat reserve which has accumulated in their tail.

On the basis of a traditional subdivision, the venomous snakes can be split up into three groups: the Opisthoglypha, the Proteroglypha and the Solenoglypha. The Opisthoglypha or 'back-fanged' snakes have poison fangs at the rear of the maxilla, and these fangs are grooved. The venom is secreted

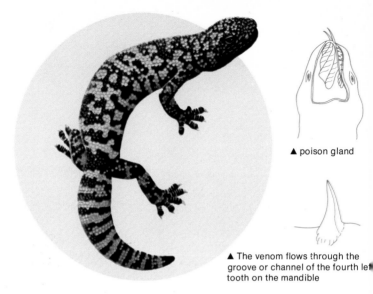

▲ poison gland

▲ The venom flows through the groove or channel of the fourth left tooth on the mandible

▲ The venomous Gila monster *Heloderma suspectum*

by a gland known as the gland of Duvernoy (after the man who first discovered it) and is connected to the poison fangs by a duct. The Opisthoglypha are members of the family Colubridae, and they are snakes in which this venomous apparatus is still not perfectly developed. In a few species the venom secreted is very toxic, and persons have died from their bites; the most notorious are the African boomslang and twig snakes.

Opisthoglyphous Colubridae are found more or less throughout the world. In Italy, for example, there are three species: the Montpelier snake (*Malpolon monsplessulanus*) is the largest snake in Italy, reaching a length of 2 metres and a weight of 3 kg. Typically it inhabits the Mediterranean *garrigue*, and is found in western Liguria, Piedmont, southern Trentino and on the island of Lampedusa.

It is very nimble and aggressive, and confronted by man defends itself by blowing energetically. Although lethal for small animals, its bite causes just local discomfort in man.

Other European Opisthoglypha are the hooded racer or snake (*Macroprotodon cucullatus*), so-called for the large dark marking on its neck, and the *Telescopus fallax*, reaching a maximum length of 80 cm, with a large head and almost uniform coloration punctuated by darker markings on the back. The last two species are more or less harmless to man.

Most of the Opisthoglypha occur on the African continent, including the small African sand-snakes belonging to the genus *Psammophis*. They are thin-bodied and feed on small Saurians, their bite does not seem to be harmful to man. The boomslang (*Dispholidus typus*) found in tropical and southern Africa, though lazy by nature, bites if attacked and injects a powerful venom which has caused death in humans, by provoking severe internal haemorrhages. The African twig snake (*Thelotornis kirtlandii*), has its large horizontal pupil which gives it binocular vision. It is likewise potentially dangerous to humans. The cockscomb snake is found in Madagascar, while Opisthoglypha are also found in the forests of South America, the Malayan archipelago, and in brackish water along the tropical shores of Asia and northern Australia. The majority of these are only moderately venomous.

The most poisonous snakes in fact belong respectively to the Proteroglypha (Elapidae) and the Solenoglypha (Viperidae).

The Proteroglypha are equipped with a large poison gland situated near the left and right temporal regions of the head. Each of these two glands, which can be taken as modifications of the salivary glands, is linked to the immovable fangs in front of the eyes. The fangs have an enclosed canal down which the venom flows. Whenever one of these snakes bites, the particular musculature with which the mouth is equipped makes the poison gland flatten. The lethal fluid is then pushed from here into the channel in the fang, and thence into the flesh of the victim.

The Elapidae include a large number of venomous snakes, which are often hard to identify because of their superficial resemblance to the Colubridae. They include the cobras, mambas, kraits, coral-snakes and sea-snakes, just to mention the most notorious members of the family. The poison fangs are considerably longer than the normal teeth, whose function is simply to grip the prey while it is being gulped down. The venom of the Elapidae is extremely powerful and lethal for man and animals alike.

Found in America, Asia, Africa and Australia, the family of Elapidae has no species at all in Europe. The best-known Elapidae are the cobras and African mambas; it is worth stressing the ability of some cobras to spit their venom up to a distance of 2 metres. This mechanism relies on the fact that in these animals the openings to the poison fangs are directed forwards. In this way the voluntary compression of the poison glands enables the venom to be projected outside by the teeth, with the mouth ajar. The venom thus sprayed may cause permanent damage to the eyes of the victim.

As far as the mambas are concerned, the most feared is the green mamba (*Dendroaspis angusticeps*), whose venom is both powerful and plentiful.

The species contained in the genus *Bungarus* (the kraits) found in south-east Asia and the Indo-Australian archipelago are all extremely venomous. They feed on other snakes and are terrestrial and somewhat sluggish in their habits.

As far as the sea-snakes – still Proterglypha – are concerned, these and the Asiatic file snake (Acrochordidae) are the only snakes that habitually live in salt or sea-water. Sea-snake poison is extremely toxic, and in man the effect of a sea-snake's bite can be rapid and alarming. However, they are not generally aggressive to man and in fact they tend to flee and will only bite if attacked or provoked. In the very few cases of human fatalities bites have usually occurred while a fish catch is being landed or sorted. Sea-snakes feed on fish and fish eggs.

Finally, the Solenoglypha are those venomous snakes in which the large fangs are fixed to a rotating maxillary bone and are tubular. The venom secreted by the large poison glands flows through the completely enclosed canals in the fangs. The venom-producing apparatus is perfectly structured and remarkably effective. As well as being extremely well-developed, the fangs adopt two different positions: when the snake has its mouth shut, the teeth are swung back against the palate; when the mouth is open, they

▼ Venom-systems in snakes

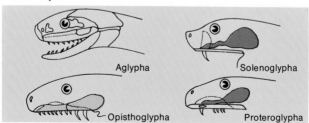

can be swung towards the victim so that they can penetrate the flesh more effectively.

This mechanism is based on the special mobility of the maxilla, or lower jaw bone, which is very short, and can rotate through 90° by muscular action.

Many of the larger heavily built vipers are sluggish creatures not prone to taking rapid flight. Some African vipers are arboreal and have prehensile tails for gripping branches; some are semi-burrowing while a few North American pit vipers are aquatic. All can renew the poison fangs, and behind each fang there is at least one in reserve, ready to go into action whenever necessary. Apart from the fact that their bodies are generally fat and thick, and the bones to which the fangs are attached are mobile, the head

▼ Poison fangs in a rattle snake *Crotalus lepidus*

of most viperids is somewhat heart-shaped and broad across the temporal region to accommodate the large poison glands which in some cases are so long that they extend down the trunk. A characteristic of the pit vipers is the presence of a heat sensitive pit between the eye and the nostril which helps the snakes detect the presence of warm blooded prey. While true vipers occur throughout the Old World, pit vipers predominate in the New World, with only two species in Asia, one in Europe and none in Africa. No vipers occur in Australia.

The venom of the Solenoglypha is generally transparent, white or amber-coloured, and can crystallize if left exposed to the air, although it retains its toxic action for some time.

Depending on the species, each snake can produce between 30 and 300 mg of venom which can be injected with a single bite. The effectiveness of the venom also varies greatly: for example it has been calculated that 25 mg of cobra venom are enough to kill a horse in a matter of hours.

From the chemical viewpoint, snake venoms are basically made up of four groups of substances: neurotoxins, haemotoxins, coagulants and anti-coagulants.

The neurotoxins act on the nervous system, which gives rise to paralysis of the various nerve-centres.

The haemotoxins and anti-coagulants can cause the destruction (cytolysis) of the liver and kidney cells, and of the inner walls of the blood vessels with fatal internal and external haemorrhages. They can also destroy the red and white blood corpuscles (haemolysis and leukolysis, respectively).

In general, the neurotoxins are the main agent in the Proteroglypha. Thus, for example, following a cobra bite, the initial acute pain at the site of the bite is followed by a feeling of drowsiness; difficulty in breathing, drooping eyelids and a progressive paralysis may ensue. Unless medical attention is available, the victim may soon die, or at least suffer severe tissue destruction.

The Viperidae tend to have principally haemotoxins and anti-coagulants in their venoms, the effect of which can be painful and cause severe swelling, haemorrhages, dizziness and vomiting.

If a person is bitten by one of these venomous snakes he should, if possible, cleanse and dress the wound and immobilise the limb that has been bitten. He should then seek medical attention as soon as possible. However it must be borne in mind that the effects of a bite from any

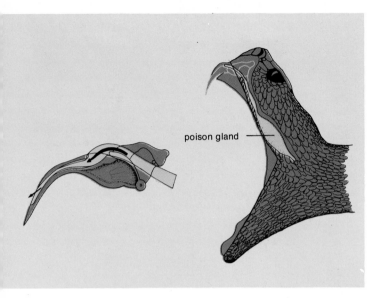

poison gland

▲ Venom-system and fang of a rattle snake   ▼ Venom-system of the Solenoglypha

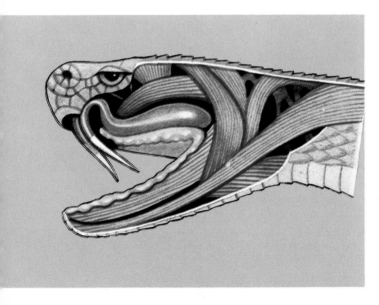

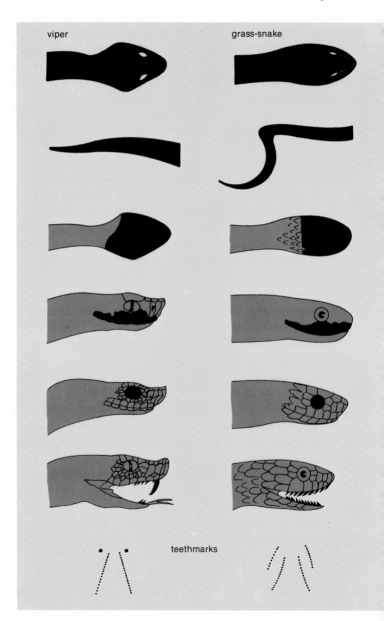

viper

grass-snake

teethmarks

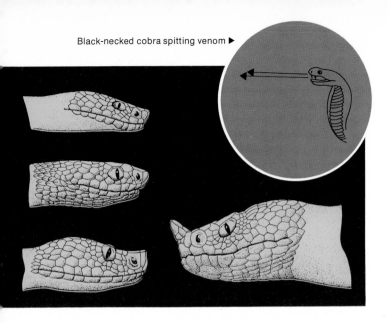

Black-necked cobra spitting venom ▶

▲ Top to bottom: adder *(Vipera berus)*; Orsini's viper *(Vipera ursini)*; asp-viper *(Vipera aspis)*; Right: sand-viper *(Vipera ammodytes)*

poisonous snake depends on the toxicity of the venom produced by the species and on the amount injected. On no account should incisions be made. In Europe the only venomous snakes, where man is concerned, are the vipers. Serum produced by a snake venom institute in Zagreb is now used widely and effectively in the U.K. in cases of serious bites from the adder (*Vipera berus*). It should be stressed that any anti-venom for use in treating cases of severe snake bite should be used only by medically qualified persons. Anti-venins are available for a large number of species that are known to be dangerous to humans.

The way in which serum is prepared is interesting. Specialists hold the snake by the head and make it bite a glass which is covered by a taut diaphragm. When the snake's fangs encounter a certain resistance from the parchment muscles contract the poison glands and the venom flows down the fangs into the receptacle. Once purified and thinned by various biochemical processes, this venom is then injected into domestic animals – usually horses – in which it will then promote the formation of specific anti-venins which are then extracted from the horses' blood.

227

Ecology

Where reptiles live

Reptiles live in virtually every part of the Earth. The various specializations with which nature has furnished them enable them, as in the Mesozoic Era, to inhabit aquatic environments, dry land, the subsoil and trees.

The most popular regions for the class are nevertheless hot, humid tropical areas, where the climate is best suited to the incubation of their eggs. The second most popular areas are the various temperate zones.

Only a few viviparous species find their way to colder habitats. Thus the North Pole is inhabited by the slow-worm, the common lizard and the viper or adder.

In America the most northerly reptile is a snake, *Thamnophis sirtalis*, the beautiful common garter-snake, which

extends into the Arctic Circle in the Yukon.

The desolate Antarctic region has no inhabitants from this class. The most southerly species are a small iguanid, the *Liolaemus magellanicus*, and a colubrid, the *Philodryas scotti*, and a pit viper that reaches southern Argentina.

As well as being few and far between in the more extreme climatic regions of the world, there are also few reptiles at high altitudes. In Europe one can find the adder and the common lizard at altitudes of up to 3000 metres in the Alps; in the Himalayas there is a viviparous rattle-snake, the Himalayan pit viper (*Agkistrodon hymalayanus*) which lives at 4800 metres, and an agamid, the *Phrynocephalus theobaldi*, which has been found at 5185 metres; in the Andes, we find an iguanid (*Liolaemus multiformus*).

229

The world's reptiles
Listed below are the various geographical regions into which the earth can be divided, and the reptilian families found within each region. Also listed are those species which have adapted to a marine life.

Palaearctic region
The Palaearctic region was once inhabited by numerous families of reptiles, but the present climate now confines most to tropical areas or at least areas south of the Palearctic region.

The order Testudines is represented by several members of the family Testudinidae (land and water tortoises), the common land tortoises, and certain freshwater species.

The Crocodylia are represented only by the Chinese alligator. The Saurians, however, are more numerous, represented by the Agamidae, Gekkonidae and Scincidae, some Chamaeleontidae, Amphisbaenia, Anguidae, Varanidae and Lacertidae. Where snakes are concerned, one finds Colubridae and Viperidae to the north and in the central region; Typhlopidae, Boidae and Elapidae to the south.

Nearctic region
Within the Nearctic region the reptiles are somewhat more widespread. In addition to the freshwater Emydidae, there exists among the Testudines, the musk terrapins, the snapping turtles and the soft-shelled turtles. The Crocodylia have just two species: the common Mississippi alligator and the common American crocodile. In the case of the Saurians, most of the species living in the Palaearctic region, such as Agamidae, Lacertidae, chameleons and monitor lizards, are not to be found here, but instead one finds members of the Iguanidae, Teiidae, Xantusiidae, Helodermatidae and Anniellidae. There are also Gekkonidae, Scincidae, Anguidae and Amphisbaenia.

With regard to the snakes, there are several species of Colubridae, Boidae, Elapidae, Viperidae (Pit-vipers only) and Leptotyphlopidae.

Ethiopian region
Within the Ethiopian region there are no marsh- or swamp-dwelling terrapins belonging to the family Emydidae; instead we find tortoises, soft-shelled turtles, and the side and snake-necked terrapins. Among the Crocodylia one finds only crocodiles. The Saurians are very numerous, with one family exclusive to this region: the Cordylidae. There are also Gekkonidae, Chamaeleontidae, Scincidae, Amphisbaenia,

Lacertidae, Varanidae and Agamidae. With regard to the snakes, there are many species such as pythons, Leptotyphlopidae and Elapidae, Viperidae (except rattle-snakes), Colubridae and Typhlopidae.

Malagasy region

Within the Malagasy region, the reptile fauna differs only slightly from that of the neighbouring Ethiopian Region.

The Saurians are represented by Gekkonidae, Chamaeleontidae, and Cordylidae, as well as Iguanidae, which are typical inhabitants of the New World.

There are no venomous snakes whatsoever, but there are a lot of Colubridae and several pythons.

Oriental region

Within the Oriental region there are quite a lot of Testudines: Trionychidae, Emydidae, and certain tortoises.

The Crocodylia include exclusive forms such as the gharial and false gharial as well as crocodiles.

In the Saurian group one finds few Chamaeleontidae, and more types of Typhlopidae, as well as Gekkonidae, Scincidae, Agamidae, Lacertidae and Varanidae. This last family includes, in this zone, the komodo dragon, the Malayan monitor, the Indian monitor and the rough-necked Borneo monitor. The Saurians of the Oriental Region also include the tiny family of Lanthonotidae. *Lanthonotus borneensis* is a strange creature which was previously classified by zoologists as a member of the Helodermatidae, and which was thought to have affinities with the snakes.

As far as snakes are concerned, the Oriental Region houses many Colubridae, Acrochordidae, Typhlopidae, Leptotyphlopidae, Uropeltidae, Aniliidae, Xenopeltidae, Boidae, Elapidae, and Viperidae. The burrowing primitive Uropeltidae (shield-tails) are exclusive to India and Ceylon while the Xenopeltidae are confined to the Indo-Malaysian region. The Aniliidae are found also in the New World and are likewise adapted to living underground.

Australian region

Within the Australian region there is one endemic species of crocodile and numerous Testudines (Carettochelydae, Chelydae, Trionychidae but no Testudinidae). Marine turtles belonging to Cheloniidae and Dermochelyidae are common.

The Saurians are represented by the families Varanidae, Agamidae, Scincidae and Gekkonidae.

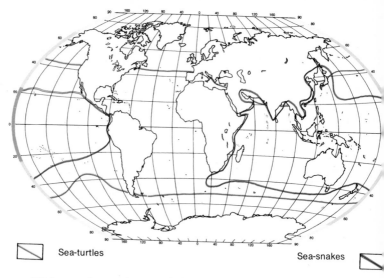

Sea-turtles

Sea-snakes

With regard to snakes one finds Typhlopidae, Boidae, Colubridae and, above all, Elapidae, in a large number of forms. There are, however, no Viperidae.

New Zealand
The islands of New Zealand, which have no snakes at all, are the only place where the tuatara lives, the last member of the old Order of Rhynchocephalia, which is otherwise completely extinct. Among the Sauria the Gekkonidae and Scincidae are common on these islands.

Neotropical region
Within the Neotropical region the Testudines are well represented with a few Testudinidae, Cheloniidae, Dermochelyidae and Trionychidae, and a large number of Chelydae and Pelomedusidae.

Among the Crocodylia one finds crocodiles in the north and caimans as well as the alligator.

The Saurians are dominated by the Teiidae and Iguanidae, with the latter including the Galapagos varieties (both land and sea iguanas) as well as some Gekkonidae, Scincidae, Amphisbaenia and Anguidae.

With regard to snakes one finds Viperidae (pit-vipers only), Colubridae, Elapidae, Boidae, Aniliidae, Anomalepidae, Leptotyphlopidae and Typhlopidae.

232

▲ A group of green turtles *Chelonia mydas*

233

Marine reptiles

It is important to mention the sea, which is inhabited by the Cheloniidae and Dermochelyidae. Among the Saurians, one finds the Galapagos sea iguana.

Relationships

Reptiles are not generally social creatures. The herd instinct, which binds individuals of the same species together, only occurs in a few species and at particularly significant moments such as in the breeding season.

The marine turtles form large seasonal gatherings in the places where they nest. At a given time of year adult females leave the sea, *en masse*, and make their way up certain beaches where they lay their eggs. They travel enormous distances between their feeding grounds and breeding areas.

Similarly, certain sea-snakes gather periodically in mid-ocean, possibly to encourage encounters between individuals of opposite sexes prior to mating. On the other hand the giant Galapagos iguanas are in the habit of living a communal existence.

The most curious cohabitating animals are the tuataras of New Zealand. It has been observed that these animals have a close relationship with sea-birds (such as petrels and shearwaters) sharing their nesting burrows. It is possible that the birds' excrement provides a plentiful store of organic matter which is ideal for the development of a numerous population of insects on which the tuataras feed.

Both crocodiles and alligators perform an essential function which is to keep open the channels in the swamps and wetlands where they live. This enables other aquatic animals to pass freely along the waterways.

Plovers are very useful to crocodiles, not only cleaning the inside of their mouths of leftover titbits and leeches, but also alerting them to their enemies.

There are on the other hand traditional enemies of both the crocodiles and other reptiles. Certain birds of prey feed on reptiles and their eggs while in England it is believed that the buzzard (*Buteo butes*) preys on adders. In africa the secretary bird (*Sagittarius*) is known to kill and eat small snakes and lizards as well as a variety of frogs, and small birds and mammals.

At the same time some species of mammal manage to get the better of reptiles. For example, the common European hedgehog, among the insectivores and the mongoose, belonging to the family Viverridae, both include reptiles in their diet.

In its skirmishes with cobras the mongoose is assisted by its thick fur, and nimble movements. It is also to some extent naturally immune from their venom. Despite this the mongoose always relies on its swift reflexes, and invariably manages to bite the snake's neck and kill it.

Many invertebrates with carnivorous diets are likely to prey on reptiles. These also include scorpions, some spiders and even giant centipedes which kill small lizards.

It is well known that driver and safari ants will devour any

▲ Tegu, genus *Tupinambis*

animal which is unable to flee from their path. They have also been known to kill large pythons after these have just consumed a heavy meal.

The diet of the European hedgehog includes adders. Not only is the hedgehog virtually immune to the adder's venom but it is protected by its prickles which are erected when confronted by an aggressive reptile.

Baboons, certain types of lemur, pigs, as well as the true carnivores such as lions and jaguars, may all feed on reptiles.

▲ A fight between an asp and a hedgehog

Reptiles and man
Man has always felt both scared of and intrigued by reptiles.
History is full of stories and legends concerning these
creatures, although the majority are often more romantic
than factual. The snakes in particular have been, and in
some cases still are, the focus of religious beliefs and are
often accredited with supernatural powers.

In the modern world reptiles are still useful to man. By
eating insects and small mammals such as rats and mice,
many of which may carry disease and destroy crops, reptiles
perform an important ecological role by keeping pests under
control. Similarly, the freshwater turtles and terrapins help
to keep aquatic environments clean by eating diseased or
dead fishes.

Some reptiles are also eaten by man. For instance, many
sea-turtles, and freshwater terrapins, some snakes (such as
pythons, rattle snakes, and sea snakes) and certain saurians
are prized for their flesh, which is considered by some

people to be a gastronomic delicacy.

The turtles also provide so-called 'tortoise shell', which is taken from the carapace of certain species. In particular, the hawksbill turtle (*Eretmochelys imbricata*) is much sought after because the coloured plates of its shell are particularly attractive. When polished, these plates are used to manufacture items such as combs, cigarette-cases, powder compacts, as well as jewellery.

Similarly, the hides of crocodiles, alligators, lizards and snakes have also long been sought after to produce fashion accessories including shoes, handbags and belts. As the result of the increasing demands of fashion, many of these animals were slaughtered on such a massive and wide scale that they were in danger of being exterminated. In recent years, however, there has been an increasing awareness of the need for conservation which has led to legislation prohibiting the killing of many of these endangered species, and a subsequent reduction in their slaughter. Each alligator handbag requires about twenty-five small matching skins. As the result of the hunting restrictions these are now difficult to obtain and consequently command a high price.

▼ A fight between a cobra and a mongoose

▲ How to handle small reptiles; the tail should also be supported

Unfortunately, the current demand exceeds legitimate supplies and this has led to an increase in poaching in recent years.

In North America the alligators are currently protected species, but some businessmen believe that it would be beneficial to both themselves and the alligators if they are allowed to establish breeding farms on a commercial basis. A few of these have already been set up, although the owners are not yet allowed to slaughter their stock to supply the tanning industry.

▼ How to hold snapping turtles

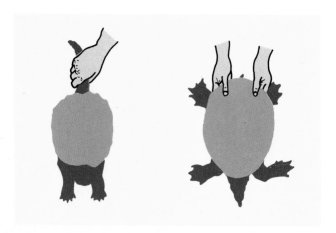

▲ Hawksbill turtle *(Eretmochelys imbricata)*

The wetlands and swamps of Lousianna, which are the alligators' natural habitat, are gradually being drained by man to make way for building developments, and so the commercial breeding farms are able to ensure a suitable environment for the alligators for a while. It has also been noted that there has been a population increase since these protected habitats have been maintained, and one argument for the development of commercial breeding farms is that they could produce an adequate supply of skins, thus making poaching uneconomic and at the same time ensuring the survival of the species.

Finally because of some of their rather unusual biological features, reptiles make intriguing and popular pets, ranging from common lizards to the more exotic and rarer species such as snakes, crocodiles and alligators.

Overleaf: Green turtle *Chelonia mydas* ▶

Classification

Summary
There are today approximately 6000 species of reptiles which have been divided by zoologists into four Orders, based on their morphological, anatomical and physiological features. The following is a general summary of these Orders, giving the basic features of each family.

Testudines (turtles, terrapins and tortoises)
These are divided into the suborders, Cryptodira, and Pleurodira. The former have the plastron covered by 11–12 horny plates, or, alternatively, the plastron and scutum covered by hard skin; the head may or may not be retractable inside the carapace, and moves on a vertical plane. The Pleurodira have the plastron formed by 13 horny plates: the head is partly protected by the carapace and can be moved on a horizontal plane. Just two families belong to the Pleurodira: the Pelomedusidae and the Chelidae; the remaining ten families belong to the Cryptodira.

Family Dermatemydidae: a fully aquatic South American turtle is assigned to this family.

Family Carettochelyidae: the sole representative is the New Guinea *Carettochelys*, a large freshwater turtle with paddle-shaped limbs and a soft skin covering the carapace.

Family Pelomedusidae: turtles with short, fat necks found in Africa, Madagascar and South America.

Family Chelydae: snake-necked turtles living in South America, Australia and New Guinea (e.g. matamata).

Family Chelydridae: includes just a few freshwater North American species (e.g. snapping turtle and alligator turtle).

Family Kinosternidae: includes the smallest American terrapins with hinged plastron (e.g. musk terrapins).

Family Platysternidae: the only member of this family lives in southern China, Burma and Thailand; it has a soft shell and a large head.

Family Emydidae: the largest family as far as freshwater species are concerned (76 species in all); they have a smooth, oval shell, and retractable head, legs and tail.

Family Testudinidae: land species with a markedly convex carapace and sturdy legs. The carapace houses the head, legs and tail, which are all perfectly retractable.

Family Cheloniidae: all but one of the large sea turtles are contained in this family. The carapace is covered by horny plates and is flattish; the head and legs are not retractable.

Family Dermochelydae: includes only one species of sea turtle, the giant leatherback turtle.

Family Trionychidae: includes forms without horny plates, which can both swim and walk on dry land.

Crocodylia (crocodiles, alligators, caimans, gharial)

There are just 23 species grouped in three families.

Family Crocodylidae: includes the larger forms with broad heads, common in Africa, Asia and South America. Fourth lower tooth is visible when mouth is closed.

Family Alligatoridae: includes the alligators and caimans which do not differ greatly from the true crocodiles belonging to the previous family except in size, and for the fact that their head is slimmer; their mouth, when closed, does not show the fourth lower tooth.

Family Gavialidae: the gavial has a very long head, designed for seizing the fishes on which it feeds; it leads a completely aquatic life in the rivers of India and Pakistan.

Rhynchocephalia (tuatara)

Just one species has survived, the tuatara, which lives only in New Zealand. Although body is lizard-like there is no copulatory organ; the teeth are fused to the jaws; the skull has a beak-like protuberance on the upper jaw; it also has the so-called 'third eye'.

243

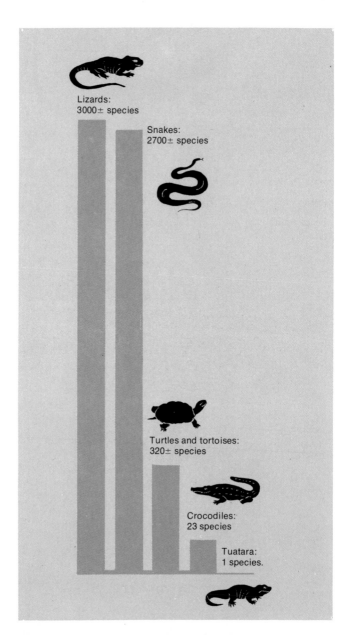

Lizards:
3000± species

Snakes:
2700± species

Turtles and tortoises:
320± species

Crocodiles:
23 species

Tuatara:
1 species.

▲ The number of Saurians currently in existence

subclass	Order	Suborder
ANAPSIDA	TESTUDINES OR TESTUDINATA	Pleurodira Crypodira
LEPIDOSAURIA	RHYNCHOCEPHALIA	
	SQUAMATA	Saurians Snakes
ARCHOSAURIA	CROCODYLIA	

Squamata

This order includes nearly all the lizards, amphisbaenians and snakes. The horny scales covering the body are cast off or sloughed; the cloacal aperture is transverse, there is a double copulatory organ, and the young have a special tooth with which they release themselves from the egg. The order can be subdivided into the two suborders: Sauria (worm lizards and lizards), and Serpentes (snakes).

The Saurians number about 3000 species, found in every corner of the world, and are divided into some 20 families.
Family Gekkonidae: small animals with flattish bodies and often strange-shaped tails; excellent climbers.
Family Pygopodidae: Australian, nocturnal Saurians.
Family Agamidae: a huge family (300 species) found in Africa, Asia and Australia, with strong legs.
Family Chamaeleontidae: includes arboreal animals with pincer-like feet, a tongue that can be evaginated, and remarkable capacities for camouflage and mimicry.
Family Iguanidae: a huge family (700 species) living mainly on the American continent but also in Fiji and Madagascar.
Family Xantusiidae: small, viviparous, nocturnal, desert-dwelling Saurians, found in the Americas and West Indies.
Family Scincidae: found on every continent; terrestrial, occasionally arboreal and often burrowing, with cylindrical bodies, and usually slender tail and reduced limbs.
Family Dibamidae: found in the East Indies and in Mexico, includes just a few limb-less, burrowing species.

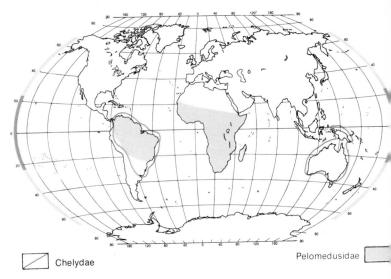

▲ Distribution of Pleurodira

 Chelydae   Pelomedusidae ☐

Family Cordylidae: An African group containing the girdle tailed lizards and plated lizards. Most have spiny tails and are rock dwellers.

▼ Distribution of Testudinata and Emydidae

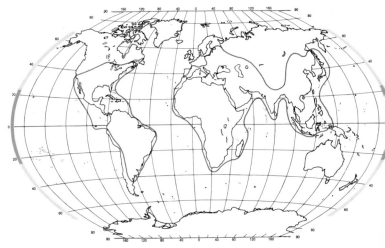

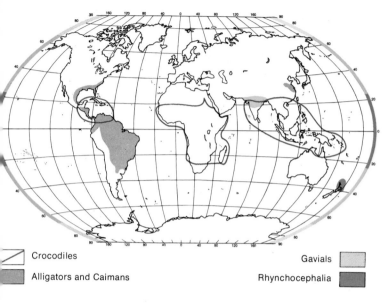

| | Crocodiles | | | Gavials |
| | Alligators and Caimans | | | Rhynchocephalia |

▲ Distribution of Crocodylia and Rhynchocephalia

Family Teiidae: this family corresponds to the Lacertidae in the New World, and have many similar features. The large South American Tegu belongs to this group. The members of this family have a snake-like tongue.

Family Lacertidae: the largest lizard family in the Old World. They are nimble creatures, with well-developed tails and legs, covered with small regular scales.

Family Amphisbaenia: closely resembling earthworms, these Saurians live underground and are found in Central and South America, Africa and Asia.

Family Anguidae: includes the slow-worm and grass-snakes of Europe, as well as the American alligator lizards that have well developed limbs and the large galliwasps of tropical America. Bony plates are present in the skin.

Family Anniellidae: burrowing leg-less species in California and Baja California.

Family Xenosauridae: two genera of crested lizards that have limbs. One lives in Central America while the other, a partly arboreal and aquatic form is confined to China.

247

Family Helodermatidae: includes the only living venomous lizards. They are restricted to dry areas in South Western United States and Mexico.

Family Varanidae: The largest known lizards belong to this family. All the species have elongated bodies and strong muscular tails. Like the Teidae they have a snake-like retractile tongue. They are confined to Africa, Asia, East Indies and the Australasian region.

Family Lanthanotidae: just one species in Sumatra.

Family Amphisbaenidae: a small group of limb-less worm lizards, more or less restricted to Africa.

Family Trogonophidae: most of the worm lizards belong to this family. They are found in Southern Europe, Africa, South Eastern United States, Central and South America, West Indies.

The Serpentes include some 2700 species. Except for Ireland and New Zealand they are distributed throughout the world.

Family Boidae: this family contains not only boas and pythons but also the wood snakes, dwarf boas and the rare Indian Ocean snakes.

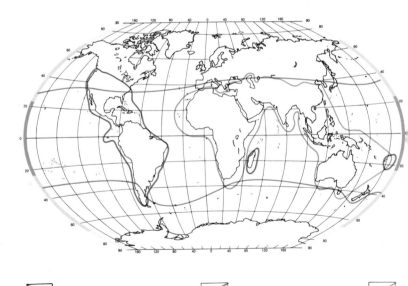

Gekkonidae   Iguanidae   Agamidae

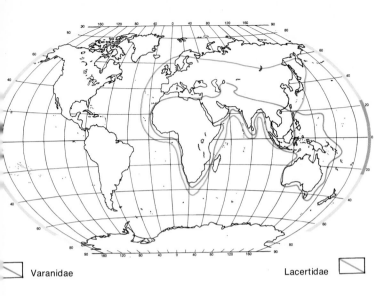

Varanidae   Lacertidae

◀ Distribution of Saurians ▲
▼

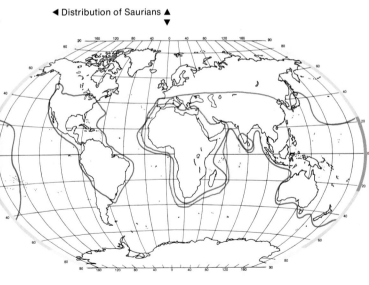

Scincidae   Chamaeleontidae

CLASSIFICATION

Family Pythonidae: it is an ancient group, exemplified by a number of primitive features, notably in the skull and in the remnants of the pelvis and hind limbs. None is venomous; they subdue their prey by constriction. The largest known snake (Anaconda) belongs in this family. Boas are primarily New World but some smaller forms occur in Malagasy, Pacific Islands and arid parts of North Africa and Asia. Pythons are exclusive to the Old World and Australia.
Families Typhlopidae, (usually Anomalepidae and Leptotyphlopidae): burrowing snakes, usually almost completely blind. They occur in warm temperate and tropical regions of the world.

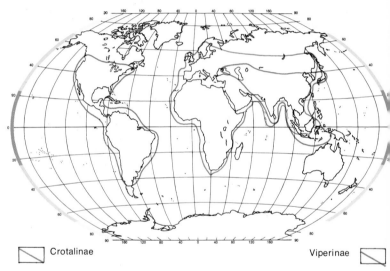

☐ Crotalinae   Viperinae ☐

▲ Distribution of Viperidae

Families Aniliidae, Uropeltidae, Xenopeltidae: burrowing non-venomous, primitive snakes; Mainly found in India, Sri Lanka and South East Asia.
Family Acrochordidae: water-snakes living in the estuaries of rivers and coastal zones in the East; they have non-overlapping granular scales.
Family Colubridae: the largest family, common in both tropical and temperate zones throughout the world. It includes harmless as well as poisonous forms.
Family Elapidae: includes dangerously venomous species,

250

living in the tropical and sub-tropical belt. Some are often hard to identify because of their superficial resemblance to the Colubridae. Members: cobras, mambas, coral snakes, kraits and sea-snakes; also includes the venomous sea-snakes, well adapted to the aquatic life; fairly frequent along the coasts of Asia, East Africa and Australia. *Family Viperidae:* includes the true vipers that live in the Old World and the pit vipers that live mostly in the New World; European species extend as far as the Arctic Circle. They have highly developed poison-systems which on the whole are very effective. Viperids are terrestrial and arboreal with a generally thickset trunk and short tail; the

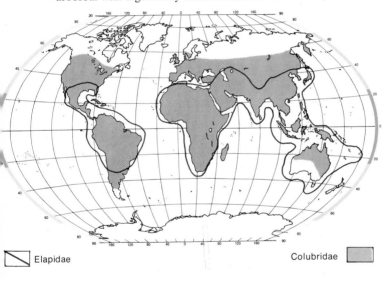

Elapidae   Colubridae

head is usually wide and triangular in shape, designed to house the large poison glands. In most species the large plates on the head are replaced by numerous small scales and the pupil is vertical. The 'New World vipers' have erectile fangs which can be folded back against the palate; they are similar to other members of the Viperidae, but differ in having the sensory pit. The family also includes a few aquatic forms, as well as arboreal forms with prehensile tails. Pit vipers live in south-east Asia and the East Indies, but the majority are found on the American continent.

251

Bibliography

Europe
Arnold, E. N. and Burton, J., *A field guide to the reptiles and amphibians of Europe.* Collins, London, 1977.
Fretey, J., *Guide des reptiles et batraciens de France.* Hatier, Paris, 1975.
Smith, M., *The British Amphibians and Reptiles.* Collins, London (5th edition), 1973.
Trutnau, L., *Europaische Amphibien und Reptilien.* Belser, Stuttgart, 1975.

Amphibians
Cochran, D., *Living Amphibians of the World.* Hamish Hamilton, London, 1961.
Deuchar, E. M., *Xenopus the South African Clawed frog.* Wiley, London, New York, Sydney and Toronto, 1975.
Noble, G. K., *Biology of the Amphibia.* McGraw-Hill, New York, 1931.
Vial, J. L. (editor), *Evolutionary Biology of the Amphibia. Contemporary research on major problems.* University of Missouri Press, Columbia, 1973.

Crocodilians
Guggisberg, C. A. W., *Crocodiles.* David and Charles, Newton Abbot, 1972.
Minton, S. A. and Minton, M. R., *Giant Reptiles.* Scribners, New York, 1973.
Neill, W. T., *The Last of the Ruling Reptiles: alligators, crocodiles and their kin.* Columbia University Press, New York and London, 1971.

Snakes
Klauber, L. M., *Rattlesnakes, their habits, life histories and influence on mankind.* 2 vols. University of California Press, Berkeley and Los Angeles, 1956.
Minton, S. A., *Venom Diseases.* Charles C. Thomas, Springfield, 1974.
Parker, H. W., *Snakes.* Hale, London, 1965.
Parker, H. W., *Snakes – a natural history.* Revised and enlarged edition by A. G. C. Grandison. British Museum (Natural History)/Cornell University Press, Ithaca and London, 1977.
Pope, C. H., *The Giant Snakes.* Routledge and Kegan Paul, London, 1962.
Reid, H. A., Adder bites in Britain. *British Medical Journal 2*: *153–156*, 1976.

Turtles
Ashley, L. M. *Laboratory Anatomy of Turtles.* W. C. Brown, Iowa, 1960.
Bustard, R., *Sea Turtles.* Collins, London and Sydney, 1972.
Carr, A., *The Turtle: a natural history of sea turtles.* Cassell, London, 1968.
Hoke, J., *Turtles and their care.* Franklin Watts, New York, 1970.
Pritchard, P. C. H., *Living turtles of the world.* T.F.H. Publications, New Jersey, 1967.

General
Bellairs, A., *The Life of the Reptiles.* 2 vols. Weidenfeld and Nicolson, London, 1969.
Bellairs, A. d'A. and Attridge, J., *Reptiles.* Hutchinson, London, 1975.
Bucherl, W., Buckley, E. E. and Deulofeu, V. (editors), *Venomous Animals and their Venoms.* Academic Press, New York, 1968.
Carr, A., *The Reptiles.* Time Life International, 1964.
Charig, A. and Horsfield, B. *Before the Ark.* B.B.C., London, 1975.
Colbert, E., *Evolution of the Vertebrates.* John Wiley, New York, London, 1969.
Cox, B., *Prehistoric Animals.* Hamlyn, London, 1969.
Gans, C., *Biomechanics.* Lippincott, Philadelphia and Toronto, 1974.
Gans, C. (Bellairs, A. d'A.) and Parsons, T. S. (editors), *Biology of the Reptilia.* Academic Press, London and New York, 1969 et seq.
Goin, C. J. and Goin, O., *Introduction to Herpetology.* 2nd ed. Freeman, San Francisco and London, 1971.
Lofts, B. (editor), *Physiology of the Amphibia.* Vol. 2. Academic Press, New York and London, 1974.
Mertens, R., *The world of Amphibians and Reptiles.* Harrap, London, 1960.
Minton, S. A. and Minton, M. R., *Venomous Reptiles.* Scribners, New York, 1969.
Moore, J. A., *Physiology of the Amphibia.* Vol. 1. Academic Press, New York and London, 1964.
Pope, C. H., *The Reptile World.* Routledge and Kegan Paul, London, 1956.
Porter, K. R., *Herpetology.* Saunders, Philadelphia and London, 1972.
Romer, A. S., *Osteology of the Reptiles.* University of Chicago Press, Chicago, 1956.
Romer, A. S., *Vertebrate Paleontology.* 3rd edition. University of Chicago Press, Chicago, 1966.
Schmidt, K. P. and Inger, R. F., *Living Reptiles of the World.* Hamish Hamilton, London, 1957.

Index

INDEX